Spenser's Pastorals

THE JOHNS HOPKINS UNIVERSITY PRESS
Baltimore and London

Spenser's Pastorals
THE SHEPHEARDES CALENDER AND "COLIN CLOUT"

Nancy Jo Hoffman

This book has been brought to publication with the generous assistance of the Andrew W. Mellon Foundation.

Manufactured in the United States of America

The Johns Hopkins University Press, Baltimore, Maryland 21218
The Johns Hopkins Press Ltd., London

Library of Congress Catalog Number 77–4540
ISBN 0-8018-1984-9

Library of Congress Cataloging in Publication data will be found on the last printed page of this book.

Plato also in the Timaeus counsels us through contemplation to make ourselves like to the beauty of the world, like to the harmony of the circular movements that cause day and night, months, seasons, and years to succeed each other and return. In these revolutions also, and in their combination, the absence of intention and finality is manifest; pure beauty shines forth.

It is because it can be loved by us, it is because it is beautiful, that the universe is a country. It is our only country here below. This thought is the essence of the wisdom of the Stoics. We have a heavenly country, but in a sense it is too difficult to love, because we do not know it; above all in a sense, it is too easy to love, because we can imagine it as we please. We run the risk of loving a fiction under this name. If the love of the fiction is strong enough it makes all virtue easy, but at the same time of little value. Let us love the country of here below. It is real; it offers resistance to love. It is this country that God has given us to love. He has willed that it should be difficult yet possible to love. — Simone Weil, *Waiting for God*

Contents

Preface

 I first read *The Shepheardes Calender* and William Empson's *Some Versions of Pastoral*[1] in 1964. The harmonious poems of pastoral seemed an intelligent retreat from the angry and visionary acts of the movement for black civil rights. As Spenser tells us in the June eclogue of *The Calender*, pastoral represents a state in which the restless, critical mind is "weand" from wandering. Pastoral reminded us that "revolutions will have need of beauty."[2] Only some years later could I acknowledge that tensions in pastoral mirrored (granted, in safely literary form) those in the contemporary world of social change. Pastoral was less escapist than prophetic when taken as a commentary on the relations between the social classes.

This book, *Spenser's Pastorals*, is about neither pastoral's escapism nor its political wisdom. Rather, four chapters show how Spenser managed to expand pastoral possibility, in part dismissing the hurly-burly of politics for the enduring patterns of human life. The fifth chapter shows that Spenser's failed pastoral, "Colin Clout," was written under the illusion that the idealizing tendency of pastoral would adequately transform the poet's discordant personal and political world. This is the perspective true to Spenser. In the course of writing this book, however, my respect for pastoral's political wisdom deepened. This preface affords a moment to show how, and to suggest that understanding pastoral's "patrician, quietistic bias,"[3] its hint of class struggle against a vision of human community, can be a steadying force today.

Two ideas from *Some Versions of Pastoral*, when taken together, explain why pastoral is so apt a commentary on political change. The first defines the writer and reader of pastoral as an upper-middle-class person whose subject is the idealized rustic, the simple keeper of sheep. (Idealizing the rustic does not preclude his suffering rough weather, physical labor, and poor food.) No driven, competitive hero, the rustic has found a home where his mind is at rest. In his simplicity and repose he is an impetus to self-criticism for the urbane reader who stands in need of correction, who is morally inferior. Here is a reassuring experience for the reader who now knows he can learn from the rustic, that there can be "a beautiful relation between rich and poor." [4] This is certainly as far as Spenser meant pastoral to go, but the pastoral impulse is attractive today because of its democratizing power.

As Empson shows, pastoral can appear to do away with social classes altogether. In accepting the shepherd, "you take a limited life and pretend it is the full and normal one." Thus you see that "one must do this with all life, because the normal is itself limited. . . . We're all in the same boat."[5] Now this emphasis on our common limitations, our being more alike than different, tends toward the desirable, if you are a socialist. Pastoral encourages us to believe that we can be liberated from the privilege and power associated with our education, our social class, our skin color. The participation of white people in the movement for black civil rights was founded on such vision of equality; the vision, however, turns out to be primarily a fixture of pastoral art, not political life.

This truth came to me participating in the minor political cataclysms of 1968 and 1969; it was present again with harsh realism in "Colin Clout's Come Home Againe," which I was thinking about in those years. Initially, I thought that *The Shepheardes Calender* and the great pastoral moments of *The Faerie Queene* would set the stage for Spenser to continue to amplify the pastoral mode. Indeed, the first three chapters of this book argue that Spenser departed radically from his sources in contemporary and ancient pastoral and invented a new pastoral language and moral landscape that could portray, not just pastoral life, but the human condition. Why did the mode seem an unfit "home" for the Colin Clout of the mid-1590s? The answer, I began to see, concerned the intersection of Spenser's historical moment with his experiences as a young poet, and then as a landowner and government official. *The Shepheardes Calender* reflects young Elizabeth's presiding spirit of optimism, and young Spenser's hope in earthly things, his anticipation of the full blossoming of his poetic powers. However, the idealizing tendency of pastoral, its pretense that the world is ordered and that human affairs will take their benign and timely course, can be outdone by life. The changed spirit of Elizabeth's court in the final decade of her reign and Spenser's exile in Ireland brought to the fore the tension between pastoral art and political reality. The central pastoral impulse, especially its capacity to liberate the best and most democratic parts of ourselves, cannot tolerate much by way of fact.

For Spenser, the mode foundered when he mingled the outlawed

Irish clansman with rustic shepherds, when he seemed no longer in-
clined to compliment Elizabeth by portraying her as a rustic shep-
herdess. The grizzled, famished marauders who creep onto the pastoral
stage from a frightening wood do otherwise than assure us that land-
owner and peasant appreciate each other. Only "safe" literary shep-
herds and fairy queens can create the illusion that our commonality,
not our class difference, defines us. Pastoral *is* a one-sided affair, "a-
bout" the people, but not "by or for" them.[6] In "Colin Clout," Spen-
ser brings the unaccommodated poor into view and expresses some
bitterness about his own situation. These seemingly unselfconscious
intrusions ruin the aesthetics of the mode, and unmask it. Shakespeare
permitted himself a glance in the direction of such ruin when, in *As
You Like It*, he has Corin refuse food and shelter to Rosalind and
Celia because Corin's master is miserly. The two women must "buy
back" the idealizing potential of pastoral by putting up money for the
farm. Thus Corin is again a good man, and the young women are
pleased with their own beneficence.

In the least charitable view, pastoral permits the privileged to play
at being poor and to enjoy it. It is not so much escapist as deluding. On
the other hand, that delusion proclaimed may well instruct us today in
the true difficulty of renouncing power and sophistication. Pastoral
exposes the paradox of the upper-middle-class egalitarian impulse, which
may be more self-pleasing than altruistic.

While writing about pastoral ideas, I have been encouraged by the
critical intelligence and friendship of Paul Alpers. Standing more at a
distance from society than I, he better knew the points of engagement
of pastoral with social reality, but, as a true teacher, he allowed me to
discover them myself.

Introduction

When, in *As You Like It,* Corin asks Touchstone, "And how like you this shepherd's life, Master Touchstone?" he is answered:

> Truly, shepherd, in respect of itself, it is a good life; but in respect that it is a shepherd's life, it is naught. In respect that it is solitary, I like it very well, but in respect that it is private, it is a very vile life. Now in respect it is in the fields, it pleaseth me well; but in respect it is not in the court, it is tedious . . .
>
> (III, ii, 11–18)

The witty sophistication of the answer, the list of rural qualities, and the point that pastoral values are relative assume an audience for whom pastoral convention is cliché, one that knows the serious dimensions of the mode so well that Touchstone's comic tone prompts understanding laughter. Shakespeare is mocking literary fashion of his day. Some twenty years earlier, neither the key words for English pastoral—"good life," "shepherd," "solitary," "fields"—nor the mode of debate would have been intelligible. *As You Like It*, written in the late '90s, provides a critique of the pastoral convention of the two preceding decades, and Touchstone's speech goes right to the heart of the central pastoral conundrum. If pastoral is "about" the simple good life, we can only know that goodness and write about it by comparing it to our own sophisticated life. Despite Marvell's conclusion in the seventeenth century that "green shade" is to be chosen over the "busie companies of men," the locus of meaning for pastoral is always in urbane society, in the comparative and evaluative judgments of complex minds.

In *The Faerie Queene*, Book II, Canto ix, Spenser's Old Melibee, a Renaissance model of the pastoral good man, tells Calidore, the Knight of Courtesie, that his stay in "roiall court" (24) taught him to love "this lowly quiet life" (25).[1] Furthermore, Melibee does not urge the knight to choose the quiet life, but, rather, to make judgments and

1

choices, to trust his own intellection. The conclusive statement in Melibee's set piece, "It is the mynd, that maketh good or ill" (30), is understood correctly by Calidore. He recognizes that Melibee is commending, not naiveté and simplicity, but self-consciousness and deliberate will. Calidore appropriately requests "some small repose" in the country for reflection, "since then in each mans self. . . . It is, to fashion his owne lyfes estate" (31). The good life is, first, not a pastoral life, but an examined life. Pastoral landscape, with its self-contained order, sequence, and meaning, does permit the sophisticated person to stand back from his established social world, at least temporarily; pastoral nurtures self-examination. Calidore does not lose his urbane language and perspective when he tells Melibee, "For your meane food shall be my daily feast,/And this your cabin both my bowre and hall" (32). He must, however, behave *as if* mean food is a feast, and a cabin is a bower.

The transformation of complexity to simplicity—the noble man or the poet at home in a rustic world of sheep and shepherds—has given the mode its reputation for artificiality. Many critics follow Samuel Johnson, who balked at the lie readers of pastoral were asked to swallow. Johnson refused to perform the leap of imagination necessary to accept the shepherd Lycidas as Milton's companion Edward King—"We know that they never drove a field, and that they had no flocks to batten."[2] In *Some Versions of Pastoral*, however, William Empson perceived the full significance of the "translation" from complex to simple, from the encumbered intellectual world of court to the purer world of country society and landscape. Pastoral permits the intelligentsia to mingle with and compare rich and poor in a rustic world that is both idealized and self-critical. For, in choosing to put on the simple, pure garments of the green world, one reveals what one cannot be in one's own setting:

> The essential trick of the old pastoral, which was felt to imply a beautiful relation between rich and poor, was to make simple people express strong feelings (felt as the most universal subject, something fundamentally true about everybody) in learned and fashionable language (so that you wrote about the best subject in the best way). From seeing the two sorts of people combined like this you thought the better of both; the best of both parts were used. The effect was in some degree to combine in the reader or author the merits of the two sorts; he was made to mirror in himself more completely the effective elements of the society he lived in.[3]

And of the self-critical aspect of pastoral, Empson says the simple man shows up his betters: "The simple man becomes a clumsy fool who yet has better 'sense' than his betters and can say things more fundamentally true; he is 'in contact with nature,' which the complex man needs to be; so that Bottom is not afraid of fairies; he is in contact with the mysterious forces of our own nature, so that the clown has the wit of the Unconscious; he can speak the truth because he has nothing to lose."[4]

In other words, pastoral permits a safe playfulness within the social hierarchy and licenses the humble man and the noble man to step out of their places. Elizabeth, the Virgin Queen, could inhabit the green world as shepherdess, fairy queen, or maiden. She could be made to mingle with her people in such a way that she could hear the "sense" of the clumsy fool while still appearing deified in her simple glory. As shepherdess, she could take "a humble example of [an admirable] quality as its type."[5]

Had Elizabeth been a king, perhaps the heroic mode would have prevailed; the proliferation of pastoral drama, lyric, and romance during the '80s and '90s substantiates the fit between the mode and its historical moment. Thus it is now commonplace for Renaissance scholars to say, as Frank Kermode did, that the publication, in 1579, of *The Shepheardes Calender*, the first significant English pastoral, "was one of the most important events in the history of English poetry, and not only in the history of pastoral."[6] Before *The Calender* was published, English poets had produced negligible pastoral; immediately after its publication and for another century, pastoral was a central mode of literary experience.

To the casual reader of *The Shepheardes Calender*, Touchstone's point about the relativity of perspectives and Empson's characterization of the mode as marrying diverse social classes in order to set in relief the healthy aspects of each may seem to miss the mark. Yet I think that, in *The Calender* (despite its peculiar roughness), these conventions make their first appearance. And, in Spenser's late eclogue "Colin Clout's Come Home Againe," the same conventions fail. In the April eclogue of *The Shepheardes Calender* Spenser calls Elizabeth his "godesse plaine" and takes her gently to task in the unquestioned security that her love sustains his world. In "Colin Clout" the beautiful relationship between rich and poor, queen and subject, is soured by historical and personal circumstance, and the comparative court perspective is abandoned to what Touchstone calls a "vile life," a life of bitter exile.

When the young Spenser, early in Elizabeth's reign, wrote in the traditional genre of youth a series of eclogues comparing moments of life to seasons of the year, his poem captured the imagination of its readers through its vitality, the originality of its conception, and the bright intricacy of its surfaces. But until the two chapters devoted to it in Patrick Cullen's *Spenser, Marvell, and Renaissance Pastoral* were published,[7] critical commentary had mainly attended to special aspects of *The Calender*. Paul McLane[8] works out its allegory, and Isabel MacCaffrey, in a sensitive appreciation of the poem, finds interest, "not in the pastoral 'matter,' but in the mode of its handling."[9]

Cullen takes the view that the philosophic basis of Renaissance pastoral is the choice or contrast between town and country, or what Frank Kermode calls "the social aspect of the great Art-Nature antithesis."[10] For Cullen the touchstone for Spenser's pastoral (and ancient pastoral as well) is a "plurality of values,"[11] an ambivalence about the choices that pastoral poses, whether they be country-city, contemplation-action, or simplicity-complexity. He connects this ambivalence with the bounds of the pastoral idea and asserts that Spenser recognizes, in *The Calender*, that aspiring poets and great men require a "higher style, a greater argument."[12] The traditional Virgilian progression from eclogue to georgic to epic, Cullen implies, limits not only the style or rhetoric of *The Calender* but the content of its debates as well.

For me, the perspective more wholly explanatory and true to *The Calender*'s own terms begins not with its allegory, nor with mode detached from matter, but with its relation to its literary sources—primarily, Virgil and the eclogue tradition; its originality in turning the language and patterns of nature to the service of human imagination; and, finally, its reflection of a particular moment in church and political history.

When Colin, in the lines from the June eclogue below, translates the pleasant site described by Hobbinol into a blessed state, the transformation from geographical place to emblematic attitude comes closer than any statement in *The Calender* to setting out the terms of the contrast between ancient and Renaissance pastoral, a contrast that is central to this study. The eclogue begins:

Hobbinol: Lo, Collin, here the place, whose *pleasaunt syte*
From other shades hath weand *my wandring mynde*.
Tell me, what wants me here to work delyte?
The simple ayre, the gentle warbling wynde,
So calme, so coole, as no where else I fynde,
The grassye ground with daintye Daysies dight,
The Bramble bush, where Byrds of every kynde
To the waters fall their tunes attemper right.

Colin: O happy Hobbinoll! I blesse *thy state*,
That Paradise hast found, whych Adam lost.
Here *wander* may thy flock early or late,
Withoute dreade of Wolves to bene ytost:
Thy lovely layes here mayst thou freely boste.
But I unhappy man, whom cruell fate,

> And angry Gods pursue from coste to coste,
> Can nowhere fynd, to shroude my luckless pate.
>   (1-16) (Emphasis added.)

Hobbinol presents the Arcadian *locus amoenus* as a harmonious place chosen by his wandering mind. His former dilemma is externalized and can be characterized in the value-laden adjectives and adverbs that Spenser links to pastoral air, wind, and ground. The wandering mind is at home in a state of simplicity and gentleness; all is calm, all is "attempered right." In speaking of the mind in this peculiar, disembodied fashion I mean to emphasize, as Melibee did, that the quality of Spenser's landscape is of the mind's making; Hobbinol's site represents a more general state of being. Colin responds by portraying his own comparatively abstract state of being. He is attacked neither by alien soldiers nor by wolves but, rather, by cruel fate and angry gods, which prevent his mind from finding a restful shade.

Spenser takes each place or site as a metaphor or emblem of one frame of mind that the mode or "garment" of pastoral might describe. The "other shades" to which Hobbinol refers represent the myriad states of human emotion, which Spenser explores in *The Shepheardes Calender* by developing other emblematic landscapes. For example, Colin's June landscape, as Hobbinol describes it (17-24), abounds with briars, night ravens, and ghosts, forming a kind of pictorial evocation of his inner discord.

Virgil's eclogues are the most significant model of ancient pastoral for the English Renaissance. In them Virgil builds a rural world that has, in the fiction of the poem, real boundaries or limits. The poet establishes distinct and opposing sites or locations; in the first lines of Virgil's first eclogue, the shepherd Meliboeus is exiled by alien soldiers from his *patriae fines* and the *dulcia arva*—the borders of his homestead and his sweet hearth. He enters, at least temporarily, Tityrus' *locus amoenus*, where his bare needs are met with shelter and pressed cheese. In Virgil's *Eclogue IX* the landscape is delineated in surveyor's terms:

> . . . qua se subducere colles
> incipiunt mollique iugum demittere clivo,
> usque ad aquam et veteres, iam fracta cacumina, fagos
> omnia carminibus vestrum servasse Menalcan.[13]
>   (4-7)

(. . . from where our hills begin / To rise, and where their ridge slopes gently down / To the stream's beeches with their doddered tops— / Hadn't Menalcas saved it all through song?[14])

This geographical limitation may be taken as a metaphor for the limitations of the pastoral mode. Virgil, unlike Spenser, takes the *locus amoenus* to be a protective, tranquil place, but it and the eclogue do not represent the whole world. Both have boundaries determined by privacy, solitude, and political necessity—the choice of an ethical existence outside of the *urbs*. These limit the range for expressing intellectual problems and human emotions. For Virgil, pastoral is a delightful but circumscribed mode.

The sources of Spenser's emblematic use of nature and his neglect of literal narrative detail are examined in chapter 1 of this study. However, because most readers of *The Calender* will have anticipated as a hallmark of Spenser's eclogue not emblem and convention but allegory, it seems appropriate here to explain the relatively unimportant role I ascribe to allegory in the poem. The brief comments I have made on the opening of the June eclogue focus the reader's attention on the surfaces of the verse—the qualitative adjectives and adverbs, the contrast between the simple coolness of Hobbinol's place and the elvish ghosts and ghastly owls of Colin's. Furthermore, nature's cycles generalized lead us to consider the relation between the summer solstice and the counterbalancing poses of the two shepherds. Spenser encourages correspondences between nature's pattern and man's, rather than between an artificial shepherd and a good, or corrupt, courtier, bishop, or governor, whose identity pastoral might disguise.

In "The Eclogue Tradition and the Nature of Pastoral," Paul Alpers suggests ways of connecting and comparing the "conventions and poetic modes" of Virgil's *Eclogues, The Shepheardes Calender,* and *Lycidas*, all in the light of Renaissance poetry.[15] Alpers begins with E. K.'s statement in the Argument to the December eclogue of *The Shepheardes Calender*. E. K. says that Colin "proportioneth his life to the four seasons of the yeare." Alpers asserts that "the idea that there is a proportion between man and nature is basic to Renaissance pastoral and represents a fundamental point of difference between it and ancient pastoral where life in nature is an ethical alternative, one possibility for the good life."[16] Put simply, a proportion exists between nature and human nature when the two are linked as "permanent realities" like "youth and spring" or "winter and rough weather."[17] Of *The Calender* Alpers says, "When we look at Colin Clout's career under the aspect of the proportion between man and nature, we see that he is a representative man, and not as the current orthodoxy has it, a culpable failure."[18] If the sixth month, June, divides *The Calender*, it also portrays a divided mind as one human reality, acceptable and to be anticipated in the fabric of human existence. In the midseason of the year the middle-aged man senses that his past may have already shaped future possibilities. Colin says so poignantly and with resignation—"*since* I am not, as I wish I were" (105)—

but his life is still in proper proportion to nature. The June eclogue ends with a delicate, touching, and utterly conventional rendering of penning up the tender lambs against "night with stealing steppes." What we have is not rebuff or outrage from nature but a very earthy consolation that links the patterns of human life to the end of the day as well as to the inevitable rising of the sun.

Contrary to what Isabel MacCaffrey suggests, the pastoral of *The Shepheardes Calender* does not vitiate the emblematic power of nature's cycles, nor does Colin Clout's life "trace for us the line of human life as it diverges psychologically from the life of Nature while remaining physically bound to it."[19] Spenser's imagery does not demand "transposition into a transcendental key."[20] The nature of Spenser's pastoral is less portentous than this. As Empson recognizes, the effect of acknowledging limitation in pastoral is to simplify life, not in order to transcend it, but in order to "see life clearly, and so adopt a fuller attitude to it."[21]

The second and third chapters of this book, a critical reading of *The Shepheardes Calender*, explore Spenser's attitude toward issues both inventive and conventional for the Renaissance humanist. In them I assume that pastoral is a "garment" the poet wears. Having defined man's relationship to nature and the poet's relationship to the vocabulary of nature, the poet uses his pastoral poetry to traditional ethical, moral, and decorative ends. In taking Spenser's nature to be a "figuring foorth" of all qualities and patterns of human nature, I am arguing , contrary to Patrick Cullen, that Spenser's pastoral rhetoric is not limited by conventional pastoral themes and issues but, rather, that it extends to the problem of how any man lives out, or should live out, common human experience.

In chapter 4, I examine the social and political context of Spenser's pastoral, and find the poetry's poise between theory and praxis, formality and plasticity, to mirror Queen Elizabeth's creative pragmatism. The religious eclogues reveal that Spenser rejects continuous political allegory based on specific personalities and theological and ecclesiastical issues; he asks, instead, how a man can live in this world and in accord with God. Spenser's moderate Puritanism confirms his lack of doctrinal rigidity.

But Colin, the very singer who ushered in Renaissance pastoral in the eclogues of *The Shepheardes Calender*, rings its changes in a lengthy eclogue of the early 1590s—"Colin Clout's Come Home Againe." Prefiguring the seventeenth-century pastoral lyric, in which the poet steps self-consciously outside of his poem and comments on convention, "Colin Clout" rends the pastoral garment. The final chapter of my book shows that circumstances have conspired to change Spenser's relation to figures in public life—notably the queen—and to pastoral language. The pretense of "oneness" between the humble shepherd and the sophisticated poet falls apart. The clash of the old pastoral attitude with Spenser's particular life situation in "Colin Clout" is evident in two significant ways: throughout the poem (and often inappropriately), a real "I" emerges to challenge the poet's pastoral mask, and non-literary facts of the quality of life in Ireland and England contradict the "facts" of pastoral convention. English and Irish landscapes barely represent the old moral stance that tells us what we are, but, rather, portray, among other things, the effects of the Irish colonial struggle upon court and countryside. Gone is the good feeling between rich and poor, queen and subject, which permitted the queen to inhabit the shepherd's world. Spenser's pastoral place is now protected by a garrison of soldiers rather than by Elizabeth's love.

CHAPTER 1

Spenser Interprets His Sources:
The Calender's Contribution
to the History of the Pastoral Idea

In his letter to Gabriel Harvey commending *The Shepheardes Calender*, E. K., the still-unidentified commentator on the poem, seems bewildered by the work he is praising. Indeed, having listed Spenser's virtues, E. K. returns ingenuously to two troublesome issues—the words themselves and the eclogue genre. The words he calls "straunge," for "they be something hard, and of most men unused, yet both English, and also used of most excellent Authors and most famous poets." To justify the genre he draws on the past for authority. Eclogue is appropriate to young poets who are like "young birdes, that be newly crept out of the nest, by little first to prove theyr tender wyngs, before they make a greater flyght. So flew Virgile, as not yet well feeling his wings. So flew Mantuane, as being not full somd. So Boccace; So Marot, Sanazarus, and also divers other excellent both Italian and French Poetes, whose foting this Author every where followeth, yet so as few, but they be wel sented can trace him out."[1] To E. K., Spenser's language is obscure, his sources enigmatic. E. K. is too close to *The Calender* to understand it as both original and synthetic. Frank Kermode makes a claim for the poem that explains E. K.'s bewilderment: "While not ignoring the charms of the English pastoral scene, Spenser brought into the tradition of English poetry the influence of every great pastoral poet of the past, from Theocritus to the modern French poets."[2]

Modern scholarship concerned with *The Calender*'s sources has generally been of the kind we find in the *Variorum* edition of Spenser, which cites specific borrowings. The *Variorum*, for example, tells us that lines 129–157 of the July eclogue "echo Eclogue VII of Baptista Spagnolo, the early sixteenth century Italian neo-Latin poet commonly called Mantuan." Critical comments—"Spenser has his own theme, and invents his own poem"—are cryptic.[3] No one has charted precisely the ways in which Spenser reads earlier pastoral poets, the ways he filters their experience through his own life and historical moment. A helpful step in developing our understanding of Renaissance pastoral, and Spenser's achievement in particular, would be to "scent out" sources, as E. K. suggests, to provide a historical as well as a poetic context for Spenser's creativity, and to assess both specific borrowings and philosophical affinities.[4] Spenser's originality emerges when we recognize that he did not merely assent to tradition but, rather, performed a dialogue with it, enriching, molding and creating a new pastoral.

Spenser had available to him as he began *The Shepheardes Calender* an established pastoral tradition that, with the exception of Virgil, included no writers regarded as major pastoralists today. To us the poets E. K. mentions—Petrarch, Boccacio, Mantuan, Marot, Sannazaro—are usually read as literary sources of later pastoral. The first task for the twentieth-century critic interested in evaluating Spenser's use of sources is to return those poets to their Renaissance status, to establish the frame of mind with which Spenser or any sixteenth-century reader might have approached them. Much of this chapter is devoted to Baptista Spagnolo or "Mantuan," his common name itself a reminder that he inherited Virgil's mantle. In reconstructing Mantuan's world view, his blending of pagan Virgilian convention with the trappings of Renaissance Catholicism, his moralizing piety, his literal use of ancient convention, we come to understand the intelligence Spenser brought to bear on the contemporary materials available to him.

The process of analyzing Spenser's borrowing from past poets is complicated because the literal sources often prove not to be the "true" ones. In *The Shepheardes Calender* there are passages translated or closely adapted from Renaissance pastoralists—Mantuan, Barclay, Marot, Ronsard. There are no passages directly translated from Virgil. Hallett Smith is literally correct when he, like other twentieth-century critics, asserts that "it now seems clear that Spenser's sources . . . were largely Renaissance rather than ancient."[5] However, I believe that Spenser alone among the Renaissance pastoralists named consciously returns to the Virgilian idea of the pastoral mode, which he uses to his own ends. The pastoral art that Spenser understands has to do not with fate, religion, poverty, and the evils of the city, as Mantuan thinks, but with the expressive power of nature's vocabulary transformed into pastoral song. This understanding links Spenser and Virgil despite their diverse views of nature's proper use. This issue is discussed in the final sections of this chapter and in chapter 3.

I begin by questioning the discrepancy between the sixteenth-century reader's assessment of Mantuan and Virgil as pastoral twins and our slight regard for Mantuan today. If Virgil was as much a touchstone for Mantuan's pastoral as he is for contemporary studies of pastoral, then Mantuan must have interpreted him differently than we do. What version of Virgilian pastoral did Spenser receive through Mantuan, and what version did he receive through Mantuan's "translator" Barclay? For this complex process of sorting out strands and techniques of Spenser's pastoral, I depend on a single poem from *The Calender*—the October eclogue. This eclogue not only takes poetry writing and the poet's career as its subject, it also conveniently talks about Virgil in language and conventions drawn directly from Mantuan and Barclay. In section iii I show, briefly, the critical way in which Virgil taught Spenser to expand pastoral.

The final sections of the chapter turn from poetic conventions and techniques to themes and poems. I account for views of nature and pastoral character in Spenser, Mantuan, and Marot, and measure them against Virgil's natural landscape—the ancient landscape that provides an alternative for life. In section iv I ask to what use each poet puts the world of biological nature, and show that Mantuan, with his Christian judgment about the paganism of Virgil, has only a superficial interest in traditional pastoral landscape, while Spenser uses the patterns of landscape to explore a Christian problem, as in the July eclogue. In section v the discussion of Marot shows his allegorical use of decorative nongeographical landscape. Finally, I suggest that Spenser, first among English Renaissance pastoralists, frees pastoral from the *a clé* tradition, and from attachment to real geographical place. He is the first to sense that pastoral can become an integral, inclusive landscape.

ii

It is difficult for the twentieth-century reader to imagine the immense popularity of Mantuan in the sixteenth century. Among available Latin poetry, Virgil's and Mantuan's were the texts chosen to commit to memory in the schools. So familiar were Mantuan's lines that, by the time of Shakespeare's early play *Love's Labour's Lost*, they had become a means of satirizing and undercutting the sophistry of the schoolmaster Holofernes. Today one might speak of his knowledge of Latin and recite "Gallia est divisa in partes tres."[6] Holofernes cites the first line of the first eclogue of Mantuan:

> Fauste, precor gelida quando pecus omne sub umbra
> ruminat—and so forth. Ah, good old Mantuan!
> I may speak of thee as the traveller doth of Venice:
> > Venetia, Venetia,
> > Che non ti vede non ti pretia.
> Old Mantuan, old Mantuan! who understandeth thee
> not, loves thee not.
> > > (IV, ii, 88–94)

Love and understanding of Mantuan are everywhere attested, especially among schoolmasters. Julius Caesar Scaliger complains (revealingly) that Mantuan's *Eclogues* are preferred above Virgil's: *hoc propterea dico, quia in nostro tyrocinio literarum triviales quidam paedagogi etiam Virgilianis pastoribus hiuius hircos praetulere* (On that account I say, there are some common teachers in our beginning instruction who prefer his bucks even to Virgil's shepherds). Another scholar testifies that "Fauste precor gelida sonet altius quam Arma virumque cano" (*Fauste precor gelida* sounds louder than "arms and the man, I sing").[7]

Who, then, is the Mantuan of Spenser and the Renaissance? It is short-sighted merely to dismiss Mantuan as a bad poet. Like the poet Cowley and other "minor" metaphysicals, his popularity reveals to us our alienation from the taste of the Renaissance reader. Two observations help explain Mantuan's popularity. First, his language was Virgilian enough—stylized, elegantly rustic; there were sheep, shepherds, brooks, and hills. Second, his heavy moralizing, the confidence that turns the Mater Tonantis of *Eclogues VIII* and *IX* (to be explored in section iv), into Our Lady of Mount Carmel, or the simplistic, homely teaching about moderation in *Eclogue V*, "Candidus, de consuetudine," seem to have adequately hidden his clumsy, unimaginative use of the pastoral genre.

He satisfied people less tuned than we toward the disunity between formal morality and actual human behavior. Remember that the Renaissance reader saw Virgil's Aeneas, his father upon his back, Ascanius in tow, household gods in hand, not as the hero symbolic of state, history, religion, and future, but as a static emblem of piety—pious Aeneas, he is called. The Good Son protects Age, Youth, and Religion. Mantuan said what people could only pretend Virgil had hinted—that pastoral poetry may appear to be pagan, but that it derives from the idea of the Christian man as pastor.

Viewed, from a generous perspective, as a poem of intrinsic value rather than as a "document," Mantuan's "Candidus, de consuetudine," a significant influence on Spenser, might be described thus by the reader: The poet explores both the economics of the professional poet and the historic and spiritual conditions that temper the artistic climate; he moralizes against avarice and chastizes his society for its sloth and absence of heroism; he finds pastoral characters convenient, one would guess, because they can tell the truth bluntly, not because they permit "doubleness" in William Empson's sense, or because their language can evoke meaning that explains or criticizes the world of the sophisticated reader. Although the themes of clerical corruption, ill-fortune, absence of heroism, kings subject to flattery, and false poets emerge, our strongest response is to the rather ugly texture of debate and argument between the two rustic speakers. The mode of the speeches themselves underscores the degeneration of social mores and personal dignity. Candidus' truculent attack on Silvanus serves to intensify the personal identity of each speaker and when, in characteristic low rustic fashion, Candidus banishes Silvanus from his sight—*vade malis avibus numquam rediturus, avare* (miser, go off to the ill-omened birds never to return)—we are convinced that lofty issues are decorative trappings beneath which lie a bitter, satiric Juvenalian struggle for survival. Here is the uncivilized base bluntness of a beggar singing for his supper:

> carmina sunt auris convivia, caseus oris;
> si cupis auditu, fac nos gaudere palato.
> (57–58)

(There are pleasing songs for *your* ears, cheese for *my* mouth; if you want to hear, satisfy our palate.)

From Mustard, Mantuan's twentieth-century editor, we know that the poet achieved some status in his Carmelite Order and conducted papal business between Mantua and Rome. He would not have experienced the paradigmatic poet's poverty. His sources are literary, an eclectic blend of Martial, Juvenal, Virgil, Theocritus, and other, not specifically pastoral, writers. Mantuan defined his version of pastoral by selecting self-consciously from available material. He couples quasi-Virgilian language with a moral (as distinct from a philosophical or metaphysical) stance. The rustic speaker of commonplace themes is his hallmark.

Although Renaissance readers call Mantuan "a second Virgil," we cannot pretend today to respond to his moralizing, or to his poetic techniques, as we might to Virgil's. He is deaf to distinctions of linguistic level—the meaning of "*altius*," or the high and low poetic language that marks, in the *Aeneid*, for instance, the differences between the world of epic simile and the world of heroic battle. He has no sense of Virgil's multilayered syntactic structures.

A comparison between the language of the opening lines of Mantuan's *Eclogue V* and a Virgilian opening shows that Mantuan could approximate simple conventions. Silvanus' words set up a typical pastoral frame and maintain a consistent vocabulary:

> Candide, nobiscum pecudes aliquando solebas
> pascere et his gelidas calamos inflare sub umbris
> et miscere sales simul et certare palaestra; nunc
> autem quasi pastores et rura perosus pascua
> sopito fugis et trahis otia cantu.
> (1–5)

(Candidus, once you were accustomed to pasture your flocks, and to play the flute in these cool shades, and to swap jests together, and to strive in wrestling; now, however, as though disgusted, you flee shepherds and rural pastures, and you betray pastoral dalliance with dulled song.)

Pecudes, pascuere, gelidis, calamos inflare, pastores, and *otia* are good Virgilian eclogue vocabulary, and the "once-now" (*aliquando solebas-nunc autem*) construction approximates the structural and philosophical conflict built into much of Virgil's pastoral work. In Virgil, *Eclogue I*, for example, Meliboeus' misery is a foil for Tityrus' happiness; in *X*, Gallus' madness is set against the lighter loves of the Arcadians. Yet the lines lack dimension and the familiar word play that entwines man and nature and takes us deeper into the pastoral world as the poem moves along.

The frame closest to this in Virgil is *Eclogue VII*, where meaning is inseparable from word painting, and rural harmony is coterminus with pastoral song:

Forte sub arguta consederat ilice Daphnis,
compulerantque greges Corydon et Thyrsis in
unum, Thyrsis oves, Corydon distentas lacte
capellas, ambo florentes aetatibus, Arcades
ambo, et cantare pares et respondere parati.

(1-5)

(Beneath a whispering ilex Daphnis lay / As Corydon and Thyrsis drove their flocks; / Thyrsis his sheep, Corydon his unmilked goats, / Both in the flower of life, Arcadians both, / Eager to sing, or to return the verse.)

Note the Corydon-Thyrsis—Thyrsis-Corydon pattern set off by the general term *"greges in unum,"* then divided among both—*oves, capellas—ambo ambo.* Note as well the specificity of Virgil's vocabulary—ilex, unmilked goats— as opposed to Mantuan's standardized landscape. The flowering of song, rustic camaraderie, and yielding flocks cohere in Virgil's rich world.

Mantuan's thin but consistent vocabulary and contrasting time sequence give way to the georgic or Hesiodic strain of Candidus' response with its evocation, not of fields, but of farmhouse and barn.[8] Here, however, georgic *copia* does not reveal plenitude in nature but, rather, serves as a foil for Candidus' envy. The *alba mulctraria, cymbia lactis, pinguia pradia* advertise the speaker's empty stomach. Virgil, in *Eclogue I* (with which this poem has obvious parallels), is wonderfully explicit about envy. Meliboeus, though an impoverished, alien wanderer, claims: *Non equidem invideo, miror magis.* (I am not jealous, I wonder rather.) His wonderment takes in the entire pastoral setting. The vitriolic Candidus does not know the word meaning "to wonder

or be amazed"; he only knows the petulant *paenitet* (I am dissatis-
fied)—a word that he repeats (28, 29).

Even when he mourns the limits of song, he dilutes and underesti-
mates the power of Virgilian convention. Dulled with pastoral despair,
a Virgilian Candidus would hang up his pipe; but Mantuan's Candidus
becomes mute as the mythological nightingale (*fiam philomela . . . mu-
tus*); he hangs up his epic arms (*arma*) and withdraws from the urban
stage (*spectacula*). Then, asked to tell *pugnas, gesta virum, proelia
regum* (contentions, the deeds of men, battles of kings)—the subjects of
Virgilian epic—he refuses, not because of the decadence of his moment
or his limitation to pastoral song (the appropriate pastoral *topos* would
be weeds growing among flowers as they do in Virgil, *V*), but because
he lacks a knife to clean his rustic pipe.

When the occasion for consistent metaphorical language presents
itself, Mantuan chooses against it. The Virgilian analogue in *I* for pas-
toral despair is Meliboeus' complaint, which poses civil discord against
ordered vines; the pastoral world holds value, not only because it is a
source of *copia,* but also because it is the single, fertile, coherent world.
The Virgilian plaint transcends its ties to single character and circum-
stance when, for example, Meliboeus' goat bears twins *in nuda silice* (on
bare flint) amid Tityrus' landscape of pastoral greenery. The reader ex-
periences, simultaneously, personal pathos and metaphysical sterility.

That the Renaissance reader did not make the distinctions I have
just made, that he fastened on morality before artistry, on the common-
place before the abstruse, is borne out when we consider that Spenser
himself was an intelligent Renaissance reader of Mantuan. Spenser read
Mantuan with care and consideration, indicating that he considered the
Italian an appropriate master for a young poet. But, having a philosoph-
ical devotion to pastoral tradition, he took up Mantuan's simple themes
with a Virgilian seriousness and largeness of mind, as several examples
from Mantuan *V* and the October eclogue indicate.

In the first lines of Mantuan's poem Silvanus accuses Candidus of
having betrayed the pastoral spirit or *otia*: *Nunc autem quasi pastores
et rura perosus pascua sopito fugia et trahis otia cantu* (4-5). The
words describe the singer's lackadaisical behavior: "*sopitus*" means
"stupefied, lulled to sleep, inactive." The idea of stupefaction could
have provided a motif for the poem, but Mantuan ignores the larger
possibilities. Spenser seizes the word, however; the first lines of "Oc-
tober" set in motion a motif of soporific heaviness—a sense of
weight, an absence of energy, an inertia, which, throughout the
poem, tempers Spenser's treatment of the fragile possibilities of
poetry, history, and, ultimately, of human heroism. The poem
begins:

Cuddie, for shame! hold up thy heavye head,
And let us cast with what delight to chace
And weary thys lingring Phoebus race.
Whilome thou wont the shepheards laddes to leade
In rymes, in ridles, and in bydding base:
Now they in thee, and thou in sleepe art dead.

(1-6)

When Mantuan, later, gives physiological reasons for the singer's sleepiness, hunger, and thirst, Spenser interprets the reasons metaphorically; the moral and cultural climate has robbed the singer of the vitality necessary to allow him to control his world through poetry. Note the extraordinary sequence and position of the sleep language—Cuddie's own heavy head prevents him from shaping or mastering his own time, thus he cannot "weary" or control the day. Further, his laxness is passed on to an audience, the "shepheardes laddes," who relied on his guiding vitalizing force. In other words, taking Mantuan's notion of stupefaction seriously means extending it to signify that the poet fails as purveyor of moral culture, as *poeta* (artist), as *vates* (prophet, seer), and as a "prick of conscience" who teaches, and moves his audience toward virtuous action.

Another section in "October" expands the dimension of Cuddie's stupefaction to the culture beyond him, and shows more precisely how Spenser, by understanding Virgil, transformed Mantuan. The eclogue contains passages taken directly from Mantuan and translated by Barclay. Spenser, Mantuan, and Barclay treat several standard satiric themes that appear throughout classical and neo-Latin pastoral: the poverty of poets because of niggardly patrons; the absence of heroic figures about whom poets can write inspired poetry; and the difficulty of finding a mode appropriate to the historical moment. Spenser uses these themes to define the function of pastoral poetry in his own world.

All three poets derive a model relationship between poet, patron, and historical moment from Virgil's poetic progression under Maecenas. This *topos* most often takes this form: Virgil wrote first eclogue, then georgic, then epic with the encouragement and protection of Maecenas; I, as poet, am at such and such a prescribed stage in my career; I do not know if I will ever sing in epic voice; times do not foster heroism. Mantuan, of course, had no direct source for this *topos* in Virgil's poetry; Spenser borrows directly from Mantuan. In the final movement of *Candidus*, Silvanus requests that Candidus sing heroic song. He replies that there are no more heroes; untaught, flattering poets merely please kings. In a final jibe at the demanding miser, he wishes him Midas' fate.

Our concern lies in Mantuan's treatment of the *ubi sunt* theme, which evokes the ideal relationship between poet and royal patron. At one point the speakers trade insults, and Candidus, the hungry poet, hammers away at Silvanus, the reluctant patron:

fac alacrem, tege, pasce, gravi succurre senectae;
invenies promptum versu et cantare paratum.
plena domus curas abigit, cellaria plena,
plena penus plenique cadi plenaeque lagenae,
horrea plena, greges laeti, gravis aere crumena.
(75-79)

(Make me lively, feed me, clothe me, succor me in heavy old age; you will find me disposed to verse and ready to sing. A full house casts cares away, the granary full, full store, and full wine jars, and full flasks, the barn full, flocks prosperous, the money bag heavy with coin.)

Mantuan then makes the point that Maecenas protected Virgil while he sang and that this good luck gave him eloquence. The Muses avoid emaciated poets who live on subsistence fare:

Tityrus (ut fama est) sub Maecenate vetusto
rura, boves et agros et Martia bella canebat
altius et magno pulsabat sidera cantu.
eloquium fortuna debat: nos, debile vulgus,
pannoso, macie affectos, farragine pastos
Aoniae fugiunt Musae, contemnit Apollo.
(86-91)

(Tityrus (so the story goes) under old Maecenas sang of rustic matters, cattle and pastures, and in higher strain, the wars of Mars, and he made the stars resound with his great song. Fortune gave him eloquence. We, the common rout, in rags, weakened by thinness, fed on mash, the Aonian Muses flee; Apollo disdains us.)

Although Mantuan draws a complimentary analogy between himself and Tityrus (the conventional pseudonym for Virgil) by making Maecenas into an old man like Silvanus, the passage shows he had only a superficial interest in Virgil. The three stages of poetic growth are there, along with the usual "higher strain"—*altius* signified a more serious, profound poetic level. Although *magno pulsabat sidera cantu* is, in syntax and vocabulary, a suitable Virgilian line, Mantuan misses the Virgilian implication that poetry, in building an integral world, can make that world echo or resound with song. Poetry transcends the poverty of daily life. Mantuan merely complains about a medieval, astrologically determined *fortuna*. Fate and the stars are against him; poetic creativity, too, is ruled by a fate outside the self. This emphasis is supported by the earlier complaint against fate:

paenitet ingenii, si quid mihi, paenitet artis,
paenitet et vitae, post quam mihi nulla secundant
ex tot sideribus quot sunt in nocte serena.

(28–30)

(My genius is offended, if I have any; it is offensive to art, it is offensive to life, after which nothing remains favorable for me in all the stars there are in the serene night.)

Barclay, in translating the Virgil/Maecenas passage in his fourth eclogue, "Codrus and Minalcas, treating of the behavior of Riche men agynst poetes," expands to 41 lines the 16-line passage that begins *fac alacrem, tege* in Mantuan.[9] The language of poverty and plenty takes precedence over the language of poetry; patron Maecenas is twice named; poetic success is attributed to astrological influence:

Succoure my age, regarde my heares gray,
Then shalt thou prove and see what thing I may:
Then shalt thou finde me both apt to write and sing,
Good will shall fulfill my scarcenes of cunning,
A plentifull house out chaseth thought and care,
Sojourne doth sorowe there where all thing is bare,
The seller couched with bere, with ale or wine,
The meates ready when man hath lust to dine.
Great barnes full, fat wethers in the folde,
The purse well stuffed with silver and with golde.
Favour of frendes, and suche as loveth right
All these and other do make thee full light . . .
Thus do some heardes for pleasure and pastime:
As fame reporteth, such a Shepherde there was,
Which that time lived under Mecenas.
And Titerus (I trowe) was this shepherdes name,
I will remember alive yet is his fame.
He songe of fieldes and tilling of the grounde,
Of shepe, of oxen, and battyles did he sounde.
So shrill he sounded in termes eloquent,
I trowe his tunes went to the firmament.
The same Mecenas to him was free and kinde,
Whose large giftes gave confort to his minde:
Also this Shepherde by heavenly influence
I trowe obtayned his pereless eloquence.
We other Shepherdes be greatly different,
Of common sortes, leane, ragged and rent.
Fed with rude frowise, with quacham, or with crudd,
Of slimy kempes ill smelling of the mud,
Such rusty meates inblindeth so our brayne,
That of our favour the muses have disdayne:

And great Apollo despiseth that we write,
For why rude wittes but rudely do indite.
(387–428)

At the beginning and end of the passage Barclay is at his rustic, Skel-
tonic best, painting a prospering English manor and an impoverished
shepherd, summing up his picture with rough aphoristic verses. In the
Maecenas passage, however, he loses touch even with Mantuan, his
model. First, so inconsequential is the progress of Virgil's poetic career
that Barclay ignores the usual equations: eclogues=sheep; georgics=fields
and herds; epics=arms and the man. Mantuan, at least, keeps order.
Second, *termes eloquent* and *pereless eloquence*, conventional medieval
praises for skillful rhetoric, are connected with the firmament or heav-
ens, but not with poetic process. At least Mantuan's Virgil actively beat
at (*pulsabat*) the stars. Indeed, Barclay's mindless imitation shows in the
ambiguous phrase "That of our favour the muses have disdayne," where
men seem to smile on the gods instead of vice versa. The passage then
shows no conscious interest in or awareness of the value Virgil assigns
to pastoral song.

Spenser's imitation of the Virgil/Maecenas *topos* in the October ec-
logue varies only slightly from Mantuan's original, but it varies enough
to betray an individual and thoughtful emphasis on poetry rather than
poverty, and poetry that uses convention, not mechanically, but in
order to find a mode for accommodating the circumstances of a life and
historical moment. One hallmark of Virgil's pastoral and of Spenser's
own relation to Virgil's pastoral is, as Alpers says, "A sense of the contin-
gency of human utterance; [pastoral] is always dependent on the speak-
er's (or singer's) situation, powers, and limitations."[10] Virgil's speakers
represent the contingencies of human utterance, but Virgil himself
teaches Spenser, by example of his own life and art, to subsume con-
tingencies. Spenser compares himself to Virgil and struggles to create
his own poetic mask, which causes him to account for niggardly patrons,
historical circumstance in which heroism has declined, and a debase-
ment of the poet's craft. But his attitude is also self-critical in its tacit
praise of Virgil for doing the "work of poetry."

Piers, who plays the role analagous to old Silvanus in Mantuan,
urges the poet Cuddie to abandon singing of "the base and viler clown,"
and proposes that he sing of "bloody Mars" or, in a somewhat lighter
mode, of "fayre Elisa." Cuddie replies by invoking the Maecenas/Virgil
topos:

Indeed, the Romish Tityrus, I heare
Through his Mecoenas left his oaten reede,

Whereon he earst had taught his flocks to feede,
And laboured lands to yield the timely eare,
And eft did sing of warres and deadly drede,
So as the heavens did quake his verse to here.
But ah! Maecoenas is yclad in claye,
And great Augustus long ygoe is dead,
And all the worthies liggen wrapt in leade,
That matter made for poets on to play:
For, ever, who in derring doe were dreade,
The loftie verse of hem was loved aye.

(55–66)

In the rendering of the convention Spenser shows that the rhetoric of
the pastoral world and the rhetoric of the poetic process can coincide.
Virgil did not "sing of flocks" but rather "*taught* his flocks to feed," a
phrase poised on the edge of allegory and signifying that poetic genius
(flock) feeds on, or draws sustenance from, nature.[11] "Lands once la-
boured" signifies the work of poetizing, like the pristine Chaucerian
plowman works; yielding "the timely eare" suggests that the poet's
career can be intuitively in proportion to or in correspondence with
nature's cycle of life. Even the participle "laboured" differentiates,
when compared with "feede," between the uncomplicated initial poetic
impulse, the taking in of poetic material, and the consequent, more
taxing, toil to perfect the craft. Analogously, "December" poses the
vernal, youthful simile "like swallow swift I wandered here and there"
against, "seek[ing] the honey bee/Working her formall rowmes in wexen
frame," a riper activity of the "sommer season." "December" also con-
firms Spenser's rich and mature feeling for growth, for timeliness, for an
arc of human experience.

　　In the third, or epic, stage of poetic development, Spenser admits
the immediacy of historical contingency; the epic poet cannot talk
personally of poetry, but must sing publicly, in a lofty voice equal to
the deeds of heroes. Hero and poet cannot be one, as shepherd and sing-
er are. Separated from the actual heroic experience he builds heroic
monuments of poetry that live on, as the motto at the end of *The
Calender* indicates—*vivitur ingenio: caetera mortis erunt* (That talent
which is inborn lives on; others die). The epic labor, for the poet,
derives from the Horatian sense of the divine poet as civilizer, en-
trusted with preserving cultural and political experience. Horace
may make light of himself as an effete intellectual snatched from
the battlefield by Mercury—*Sed me per hostis Mercurius celer/
Denso paventem sustulit aere/Te rursus in bellum resorbens* (But
swift Mercury in a thick mist, bore me into the air through the
enemy . . .),[12] but majestic poetic heroism rings out in the final lines
of Ode XXX, Book III:

Exegi monumentum aere perennius
Regalique situ pyramidum altius,
Quod non imber edax, non aquilo impotens
Possit diruere aut innumerabilis
Annorum series et fuga temporum . . .
                              (1–5)

(I have built a monument more enduring than brass, and higher in structure
than the pyramids of kings, which not corroding rain nor the headstrong
wind may destroy, nor the sequence of years and the flight of time . . .)

Spenser, too, assumes that heroic song, the highest song, should have poet-
ic force equal to the life of the social organization it mirrors, but, when
"worthies liggen wrapt in leade," contingency sends one into the private
world where "pastoral of the self"[13] becomes the sole potentially satis-
fying option and the "hurtlesse pleasaunce" becomes the sole landscape.

iii

The radical transformation Spenser works on Mantuan's poem is an il-
lustration of his ability to understand the resonance and possibility of pas-
toral vocabulary and ideas. Such words as "timely," "laboured," "yield,"
and "feede" reveal the poet's deep desire to fulfill his own creativity ap-
propriately and to assess correctly the moral needs of his compatriots. In
The Calender, "October" alone asks "O pierlesse Poesye, where is then
thy place?" and answers with a brief, unsatisfying sojourn out of the pas-
toral and into the genres of epic and drama. All the *Calender*'s other poems
are a demonstration of the appropriateness or timeliness of Spenser's sing-
ing in the humble, safe, pastoral mode, of his acceptance of contingency.

In order to understand this mature and intelligent acceptance of
contingency, we must turn directly to Spenser's reading of Virgil and
his critical perception that Virgil shows the way to expand the pastoral
world. In "October" he calls Virgil "Romish" and specifies that he left
pastoral through Maecenas, that the conjunction of poetic powers, pat-
ronage, and heroes allowed him to complete a process of becoming Ro-
man and public. On the other hand, in his own struggle for poetic
selfhood, the young Spenser sees that heroes are lacking—mighty man-
hood has given way to a bed of ease; patrons are no longer to be found
in "prince's palace," though that is the place "most fitt"; only individ-
ual poetic powers survive. Spenser's deep understanding and admiration
of Virgil's art leads him to ask how, given the contingencies of his own
situation, he can write a lofty poem on an exalted theme appropriate to
his pastoral choice. How can he attain the high seriousness of *Eclogues IV*
and *V* or *IX* and *X*?

Virgil's *Eclogues* provide two models for "elevated" pastoral; Spenser understands the differences between them. In Virgil *IV*, *V*, and *VI*, the first model, the poet remains within the pastoral mode but sings *paulo maiora* (a little higher). The Muses are evoked to sing forests worthy of consuls; not *all* trees are humble.[14] Thus private pastoral language can celebrate the prophetic birth of a baby destined to be a public and heroic figure. In *V*, perhaps the "highest" pastoral in the cycle, Virgil celebrates the death and deification of Daphnis, the rural figure said to have invented pastoral, who is a civilizing force in the forest. He uses all nature's poetic resources to make a human death universal and cathartic. *Eclogue VI* makes explicit the choice to sing in honor of public heroes in the pastoral mode, to use mythological pastoral as an offering to the hero. In the frame, Virgil addresses Varus, a patron and a jurist in the area of Virgil's farm in Mantua:

> nunc ego—namque super tibi erunt qui dicere laudes,
> Vare, tuas cupiant et tristia condere bella—
> agrestem tenui meditabor harundine Musam.
>
> (6-8)
>
> (Now Varus, I [since there are poets enough /To celebrate you and your tragic wars]/Shall court my rustic Muse on a tenuous pipe . . .)

Virgil's model, then, expands the limits of pastoral rhetoric in order to sing of any or all human experience. Spenser follows his October poem—his questioning of the limits of pastoral rhetoric—with "November," which demonstrates the fullest depth and breadth of the pastoral mode. More personal, private, and intimate than the poem of Daphnis' apotheosis, Spenser's November eclogue nonetheless draws emotional response from the reader, not solely because of our love for Dido, but also because "thilke sollein season sadder plight doth ask," as Colin tells Thenot. Making the experience of the poem as significant as that of the individual death depends on the poet's ability to proportion the linear flow of a human life to the cycle of nature. Virgil suggests to Spenser that the expansion of pastoral rhetoric derives from a vision of nature's patterns as universal patterns and possibilities.

The second model that Virgil provides exposes the limitations of pastoral for the ancient poet. In Virgil *IV* the prophetic birth of the baby and the idealized return to a pristine golden past that follows represent the largest and most portentous political vision that pastoral allows; it is not, however, in touch with the personal kind of political and historical reality that intrudes in Virgil *IX* and *X* through the presence of two nonpastoral figures—an unidentified *advena* (stranger, alien) and the sometime poet, sometime soldier Gallus, who can only wish that he were Arcadian—*utinam ex vobis unus vestrique fuissem.* In *IX*, as they walk along the road, Moeris tells Lycidas that a stranger has seized his farm, and we, who thought Arcadia the only world, must accept its literal and psychological boundaries. Bluntly, Virgil pits the now fragile pastoral song against the force of arms. Pastoral song has lost its power to order and control experience:

> . . . sed carmina tantum
> nostra valent, Lycida, tela inter Martia, quantum
> Chaonias dicunt aquila veniente columbas.
> (11–13)

(But a poem is as successful in a place of arms / As holy doves are when the hawks appear.)

At the end of *Eclogue I* Tityrus invites the wanderer Meliboeus to share the protection of his rustic home; in *IX* the wanderers, their destiny seemingly shadowed by the sepulchre they pass, simply walk off the stage into uncertainty as the rainy evening draws on. Virgil leaves us with a single constant—the fellowship between two men. *Cantantes ut eamus, ego hoc te fasce levabo* (to keep us singing, I shall take your load), says Lycidas. Instead of informing the landscape with pastoral song, song grows softer and then diminishes, subordinated to the human landscape of the dispossessed duo.

In *X* Gallus speaks in his own (and the poet's) voice of a moment in military history contemporary with the poem and, in bemoaning the absence of a loved woman, claims that, although he would have the pastoral songs of the Arcadians assuage his suffering, his *insanus amor* (mad love) has burst through predictable pastoral and natural patterns, rituals that could contain grief. In contrast to Alexis (of *Eclogue II*), whose love lament is muted and finally overpowered by the work of the pastoral world—there are vines to be pruned, baskets to be woven—Gallus subordinates all to love, and turns his energy toward the public, heroic world that his love inhabits, suggesting a profundity of emotion beyond that which the pastoral world can contain. In the lines addressed to his woman the harsh, stark, uncontrolled pain of love pierces, and, ultimately, undercuts pastoral harmony:

> tu procul a patria—nec sit mihi credere tantum—
> Alpinas, a dura, nives et frigora Rheni
> me sine sola vides . . .
> (46–48)

(Hard-hearted, distant [can this be?] you stare / At Alpine snow fields and the frosty Rhine / Without me.)

In the lines immediately preceding these, Virgil has significantly con-
nected the energy of love with the energy of battle:

> nunc insanus amor duri me Martis in armis
> tela inter media atque adversos detinet hostes . . .
> (44–45)

(Instead mad love of brutal Mars detains/Me fully armed where hostile weapons
fly.)

Historical circumstance, contingency, and a necessary restraint prevent
such a conjunction in Spenser; he must not allow the transforming
power of pastoral song to die.

In *The Calender* Spenser stops short of the world of Virgil *X*, but he
expands beyond rustic, simple pastoral. This is critical. He chooses Vir-
gil's first model; there is no heroic Gallus for whom alien songs must be
sung (*carmina sunt dicenda*). In the elevated mode of Virgil *V*, Spenser
expands the November eclogue to include love of Dido as the moving
force of the pastoral world—a love that is cosmic in comparison to Colin
Clout's love for Rosalind as it appears in "January," "April," June," and
elsewhere. In "October," love, named "the tyranne fell," complicates
Spenser's poetic process ("unwisely weaves, that takes two webbes in
hand"), but because Spenser's pastoral world is the only world, poetry
and love survive. Love does not simply turn to madness.

Virgil limits the pastoral world because the expressive power of
nature in private life has its limits. Vegetative vocabulary diminishes
heroes and opposes the nature of the *locus amoenus* to arms and the
man. Spenser, too, understands that pastoral is limited as the natural
world is limited, but he cannot dismiss lowly pastoral—*ite domum sat-
urae, venit Hesperus, ite capellae*—as Virgil finally does. If we accept his
complaint in "October" then we must accept his deceptively simple con-
clusion that his place is to pipe contentedly in "humble shade." But
"humble shade" means for Spenser a mode in which nature's patterns—
landscapes, seasons, growth, harvest, death—can be made to fully expli-
cate the life of man.

"October" looks backward, nostalgically, to the spring of the year and
the poetic cycle, when once Cuddie led the merry shepherds' lads; it also
suspends itself in time, portraying a frustrating and paradoxical harvest
sense of simultaneous death and fruition. But "November" proclaims an
acceptance of life's cycle, a joy in embracing death harmoniously *and*
in the pastoral mode. "November" is the mode of accommodation;
"December" supports our notion that Spenser's pastoral choice is to
expand pastoral to its limits. In that eclogue, Colin, the speaker at the
beginning and end, deepens our sense of the flock as a rich, expressive

reflection of the poet's self-acceptance and his acceptance of the personal mode. He pens the flock up ruefully as the calendar cycle ends; the key word is "timely."

> 'Gather ye together, my little flocke,
> My little flock, that was to me so liefe:
> Let me, ah lette me in your folds ye lock,
> Ere the breme Winter breede you greater griefe.
>> Winter is come, that blowes the balefull breath,
>> And after Winter commeth timely death.
>> (145-150)

iv

The overtly religious eclogue—"May," "July," and "September"— are, I think, the least interesting poems of *The Calender*. Yet they do tell us something extremely important about the relationship between Virgil, Mantuan, and Spenser, about Spenser's need for poetic support, and about the beginnings of his healthy independence from it. "July" is least Virgilian, though it treats the motif of nostalgia for the golden world. Curiously, of all the eclogues, it borrows most heavily and directly from Mantuan *VII* and *VIII*. With no Virgilian model in mind, Spenser cannot maintain linguistic depth, thematic unity, or a coherent pastoral vocabulary sufficiently broad to talk about religious and ecclesiastical problems without blending imprecisely the worlds of pastor and pastoral.

In the religious eclogues Spenser may appropriately call Moses "a shepherd . . . meeke and mylde," or Abel a man "simple as simple sheepe." But imitation of Mantuan's phrases also leads him to place in one pastoral world "holy hills sacred unto saints"; Christ in the guise of "great god Pan," "Our Ladyes Bowre," holy Fauns and Nymphs sporting in the Kentish Medway, and a shellfish dropped on the head of Bishop Grindal. Clearly, Spenser thought he was writing fit pastoral; the justification may have come from Mantuan, who judges Christian moral responsibility to outweigh what twentieth-century readers call "poetic decorum."

First, what happens in Mantuan's pastoral world? In *Eclogue VII* two rustic speakers, Alphus and Galbula, discuss the most recent news— Pollux, another shepherd, having seen an *effigies* (a vision of a goddess), has hooded himself and retreated to a cloister. Or, rather, he has been transported almost involuntarily—*ferunt illum, pecudes dum solus in agris pasceret* (They bore him off while alone in the fields he pastured his flock). The two speakers then discuss God's specially protective relationship to shepherds. Galbula tells the story of Pollux' vision, boldly modeled after Aeneas' encounter with his mother, Venus, in the *Aeneid*

(*I*, ll. 330ff.). The eclogue maintains, to use the phrase of Marvell's mower, that "The gods with us do dwell"; that is enough of knowledge. Shadows deepen; the poem ends with the affirmation of continuity in the rustic pastoral world—*ipse pecus ducam, mihi pars erit ista laboris* (I myself will lead the flock homeward; this will be my share of work).

Eclogue VIII, from which Spenser borrows the debate between upland and lowland shepherds as it appears in "July," continues the exploration of Pollux' vision. The heat of the dog star causes Candidus, a fellow shepherd, to praise the cool pleasures of the mountains, and to assert, in response to Alphus' questioning, that the mountains supply not only resources for the city (marble, gold, herbs) but also a healthy environment for shepherds and flock. But when Alphus inquires about mountain religion and Pollux' reputed vision of a Nymph (from the previous poem), his lapse into pagan mythology is corrected. Pollux saw the *Tonantis Mater* and learned from her, as Adam learned from Raphael in *Paradise Lost*, the powers of the stars and of the virgin goddess (*sidera, numina prisca* l. 91). Indeed, if the virgin wishes to look with favor on the pastoral world, she can, alone, preserve it from harm. Even Aeolus, complete with his Virgilian epithet, *aequoreis ventos qui frenat in antris*, obeys her. (It is Aeolus who holds back the winds in his seay cave.) Inscribed in marble before the altar is a prayer asking the protection of the *Diva gubernatrix hominum, custodia vatum* (the goddess, ruler of men, guardian of poets). Alphus asks how a rustic might praise her and receives a list of holy days. But the abrupt onset of evening prevents a full recital.

If we measure Mantuan's seventh and eighth eclogues by our Virgilian touchstone—a pastoral life in nature represents one ethical alternative of how to live among many—we see that Mantuan's religious poems do derive from at least a token choice to defend the *rura* against the decadent city, to create biological and geographical places, to spell out with a sensitivity close to that of his *Eclogue V* the economic realities of peasant existence, and to establish, amid the ecstatic visions, a sense of workaday social life absent from Spenserian pastoral. But Mantuan fails Virgil through his inability to transcend this superficial matter of pastoral. This failure may derive from a Christian sense of security. God's universe is given; there are no questions to be asked about nature's conformity to it or about natural human conflicts brought to light in the presence of endurance, suffering, and even celebration. Mantuan creates a real rustic life, but not an examined one.

On the other hand, we can take as a touchstone what Alpers has called "the idea basic to *Renaissance* pastoral—that there is a proportion between man and nature. . . . In Renaissance pastoral with its Christian perspective, man's life has by definition a significant relation to nature."[15]

it appears that Mantuan again falls short. In *Eclogue V*, for example, we have noted that stars and fortune explain life's patterns and outweigh either the Virgilian political contingency (protection by a Maecenas) or the Spenserian acceptance of a life cycle modeled in accord with organic patterns established by God for all His creatures.

In *Eclogues VII* and *VIII* the Christian perspective sets unquestioned, rigid rules for viewing the world. Mantuan finds no validation in nature's patterns for the rightness of Pollux' vision and subsequent departure for the cloister, nor does he question in any way the discordant abandonment of classical pastoral life in exchange for religious life. Rather than play with the analogy or simultaneity basic to Christian pastoral between the simple life in nature and the most holy Christian life, he ignores it. He claims no artist's prerogative, choosing not to question, as Virgil would, the efficacy of the pastoral poetic landscape as a mode of expression or to hold in reverence, as Spenser would, the pastoral poet's labor—to order and make understood through formal song the experience of life. Not nature, or God in accord with nature, or the poet in accord with either one, but the omnipotent Godhead determines Pollux' future course of life from the first lines of the first speaker:

> Galbula, quid sentis? Pollux doctissimus olim
> fistulican *subito quodam quasi numine tactus*
> destituit calamos, tunicas, armenta, sodales . . .
> (VIII, i, 1-3)

> (Galbula, what have you heard? Pollux once the most learnèd flute player suddenly as though touched by the godhead, abandoned pipe, tunic, herd, companions . . .)

The Christian and Spenserian connection between *pastor* and pastoral, then, is in some ways irrelevant to Mantuan. The series of examples showing that God favors shepherds and culminating in the recital of Pollux' vision fails, surprisingly, to exploit the expected allegorical implications of the Lord as Shepherd or the shepherd as keeper of the heavenly flock. Indeed, the explicit statement—God called himself a shepherd *(pastorem Deus appelavit)*—seems a rote rendition of Biblical language rather than a creative attempt to humanize and simplify God or to elevate the shepherd and make him complex.

Pollux puts away the accouterments of pastoral; then, at a later time, he puts on the religious hooded robe *(bardocuculatus caput)*, having cast aside his former existence. As Pollux the shepherd he is not godly, but must become so (thus he will be Pollux, *religiosus*). Indeed, there is heavy emphasis on this disjunction. Alphus and Galbula play

pretentious dolts, posing as *rus*, rejoicing in the splendor of the paint-
ings on the temple walls in the city, and then conceding that, with all
these wonders, simple rustic Pollux could not help but see the Godhead:

> . . . nuper ab urbe
> rus veniens picto perlegi haec omnia templo.
> sunt pecudes pictae, parvi sub matribus agni
> in tellure cubant, ingens equitatus ab alto
> monte venit, radiant auro diademata divum
> et suspensa tenent vaga lumina praetereuntum.
> non igitur mirum noster si numina Pollux
> vidit.

(42–49)

(Once, I, a rustic, coming from the city, read all these things painted on the
temple wall. There are flocks depicted, small lambs are lying on the ground be-
neath their dams; a great cavalry comes from the high mountains; the headresses
of the gods are shining with gold and they hold transfixed the wandering eyes
of those going by. It's no wonder that our Pollux saw the Godhead.)

Pollux the shepherd has no intrinsic, special relation to truth or to God,
nor is he synonymous with Pollux the holy man.

Indeed, the ethical separation between Christian and pastoral shows
up in an unconscious attitude of class bias in the eighth eclogue. The
pastor/pastoral analogy is irrelevant because Mantuan resists even the
notion that simplicity hides what is really complex. Mountain dwellers,
the equivalent of shepherds here, are extolled not as simple and holy
but as hard-laboring, unspiritual animals—a youth work force. They are
*robustus iuventus, lata pedes, callosa umeros, nervosa lacertos, hispida,
dura manus* (Hearty youth, broad of foot, with calloused shoulders, sin-
ewy arms, hirsute, with hardened hands). These are true peasants, not
wonderful clowns full of arcane insight. They merely repeat the tales of
the elect—Candidus tells Pollux' story, and that with self-conscious
lacunae: *omnia non memini (mens est mihi debilis) ista* (I don't remem-
ber all of it. I'm not very smart). And even this standard modesty *topos*
must be undercut. Mantuan fears being thought not to have the proper
credentials. Thus, when Candidus suggests that it is the rustic's true
function to give praise (*'crates'*), he gets reprimanded by a marvelous,
status conscious Alphus, who squirms at an unpolished accent: *Rusticus
es, 'Crates' etenim pro 'gratibus' inquis* (You're a dolt; you say "tanks"
for "thanks"). Mantuan, a product of the elaborate sophistication of
quattrocento Italy, has not understood the romantic notion of the prim-
itive, simple man being the ingenuous, artless knower whose environment
provides the evaluative framework for understanding his own existence.
For him, the pastoral figure must submit himself to Christian missionaries.

A further example of the absence of sensitivity to the meaning of pastoral figures is in the appearance of the *Mater Tonantis* in the guise of nymph qua Venus playing her role from the *Aeneid*. Simplistic Christian morality and Virgilian language and imagery intermingle. She offers a domestic aphorism:

est facile incautos offendere. par parvulus infans
innocuous rutilim digitos extendit in ignem
nec nisi iam laesus vires intellegit ignis.

(99–101)

(It is easy for the heedless to be harmed. The little baby sticks an innocent finger in the red-glowing fire, and not unless once burned, does he learn the power of fire.)

But the aphorism comes after Mantuan has established classical credentials by "citing" the model pastoral poet, Virgil. Venus' appearance is among the most breathtaking events in *Aeneid I*. Mantuan has the nymph ask: *Care puer, quo tendis iter?/vestigia verte* (Dear boy, along what green path do you go?). Venus asks Aeneas: *sed vos qui tandem, quibus aut venistis ab oris,/quove tenetis iter?* (But who are you, or from what shores do you come, or where are you going?). Mantuan's phrases merely clothe the Christian missionary in a thin pastoral veil and justify, for Mantuan (and apparently for the Renaissance reader), the introduction of a transparent Carmelite Venus in sheer violation of the pastoral spirit. She defines values for men clearly not of her constituency to whom she, the erotic spirit, recommends retreat from the pastoral world. Into the cloister of Mount Carmel, Pollux follows the undercover goddess of love, abandoning the *crudelis Amor* of his youth. She is imposed on the landscape but her presence cannot transform or sanctify it as classical Venus' actually does. Tellingly, pastoral tranquility must be sanctioned, in the end, not by ecumenical simplicity but by urban authority and the conventional medieval authoritative book:[16]

Quod nos in pecudes, in nos id iuris habent di;
hoc rus scire sat est, sapiant sublimius urbes.
sic docuit rediens aliquando ex urbe sacerdos
Iannus et in magno dixit sibi codice lectum.

(VII, 152–155)

(What we have in flocks, the gods have in our laws. This is enough for a country dweller to know. The city dwellers may know more lofty matters. Thus Janus, the priest, once taught returning from the city, and he said he read it himself in the great book.)

In the July eclogue Spenser's imitative pastoral begins its change into confident and original poetry. Although this poem has some confusion and is not as skillfull in structure and word choice as the best of the cycle, it transforms Mantuan's simplistic ideas into an engaging complexity. In Mantuan's seventh and eighth eclogues a fairly consistent structure and set of ideas derive from the competing attractions of mountains and plains. This contrast Spenser takes as the dominating problem of the July eclogue. Mantuan holds that mountains are the holiest of places because they are the dwelling places of *caelicolae*, or sky deities.[17] They are healthier, purer, and closer to heaven. Spenser, however, cares not for the physical attributes of either site; he prefers the true lesson to be drawn from the contrast between low and high places. Such a contrast is a fact of nature's landscape and, in metaphoric guise, represents two perspectives on human endeavor, both of which face human beings. Commendable lowland humility can also be passivity or laziness; striving upward can bring both delight and knowledge. Furthermore, Spenser easily associates the conventional attributes of pastoral character with the representative Christian man; thus Christ and Old Testament figures appear as *pastores*, shepherds, and exemplars. Unlike Mantuan's doltish rustics, Thomalin and Morrell, Spenser's rustics need no missionaries to teach them the language of Christian pastoral. Spenser exploits the highland/lowland framework by using the qualities of geographical place and by rising above them to the qualities of moral existence.

Qualities of geographical place, for Spenser, are features of the landscape such as the grassy bank, the bushes, and the hill and plain of the July eclogue, but his interest in them lies, not in the *flora* and *fauna* they produce or in the detail and individuality of their particular beauty, but in their symbolic potential to characterize a state of mind. Thus the admitted fascination with nature appears to be extrinsic to nature herself. The poet wonders at the life cycle of a flower, quickening from a seed to bloom and die, or at the pattern of the seasons, because these patterns explicate the course of human life. These godly patterns make accessible to the human mind, as Mantuan's *Fortuna* did not, a rich opportunity to observe, to choose, to analyze, and to mold one's own experience.

The "plot" of "July" is quite simple. Thomalin, a jolly shepherd, is urged by Morrell, a proud goatherd, to exchange the lowly plain for the more holy mountain. Thomalin claims that righteous humility, simplicity, and trust in God characterize the man who lives in the dale, while ambitiousness and proud climbing signify the man who lives aloft. He gives, as arguments for a lowland home, the exemplary, simple lives of the first shepherds who, by contrast with the wealthy, corrupt and greedy potentates of today, lived in the sight of god. Morrell asserts that available riches mean good health, not greed; he shows limited sympathy with Algrind (Elizabeth's Bishop Grindal), who was taught to love the low degree because while sitting upon a hill he was injured by an eagle, which dropped a shellfish on his head. The poem ends without concluding.

In the first lines of the eclogue Spenser seems to be reading Mantuan upside down. Proud Morrell, whose herd strays into the bushes below him, tries to convince Thomalin that he and his flock would be better off coming up the hill. Thomalin refuses the offer to climb in strong, moral language:

Ah God shield, man, that I should clime,
    and learne to looke aloft,
This reede is ryfe, that oftentime
    great clymbers fall unsoft.
In humble dales is footing fast,
    the trode is not so tickle:
And though one fall through heedlesse hast,
    yet is his misse not mickle.
(9-16)

However, when we look closely at Thomalin's argument, we discover that he is condemning, not the morality of climbing, but, rather, the dangers. Conventional, practical wisdom (reede=motto; ryfe=common) tells us that the higher you are the more it hurts when you fall. Furthermore, falling on account of "heedlesse hast" is not revenge wrought on the climber. Thomalin clearly indicates that the lowland dweller can be hasty too. We are not in Mantuan's simple moral universe.

Morrell counters Thomalin's refusal to climb with, among others, the complex and bold argument (bold because Spenser treats it seriously) that says Thomalin is afraid to climb because of the havoc wrought by the first fall:

Whilome there used shepheards all
    to feede theyr flocks at will,
Till by his foly one did fall,
    that all the rest did spill.
And sithens shepheardes bene foresayd
    from places of delight . . .
(65-70)

We should note, as well, the word "delight," and the ensuing contrast between Morrell's charming lyric tone and Thomalin's brusque, plain voice tempt us to take the climber's position.

Let me hint at the theological problem, often called the "paradox

of the fortunate fall, " that emerges in "July"'s exploration of both
high and low. It states, simply, that, had man not fallen from innocence,
Christ, the manifestation of God's love of man as body and spirit, would
never have been incarnated, and man would have remained, in a pro-
found way, ignorant of the omnipotence and benignity of his maker.
Though the fortunate fall is the paradigm of the problem, its questions
reappear each time man weighs for himself the risks and values of being
a Faustus, an "overreacher," every time he weighs the possibility of being
nearer to God, of being exalted by a combination of knowledge and faith
and not simply by faith alone. Is the hill dweller, then, to be condemned
unequivocally for his striving?

This paradox emerges on every level in the eclogue. Spenser balances
Thomalin's recital of the plain virtues as they appeared during the gold-
en age and mountain ideals represented by present-day landscape (holy
hills, nigher to heaven). But reality also includes history. The decline
of virtue has transformed nature so that the lowland represents not posi-
tive virtue but minimal vice, and the upland represents not vice but merely
the dangers of it. The hills *are* attractive in Spenser's eyes. He gives them
the best poetry of the eclogue, stirring the reader's imagination:

> Besyde, as holy fathers sayne,
>   there is a hyllye place,
> Where Titan ryseth from the mayne
>   to renne hys dayly race.
> Upon whose toppe the starres bene stayed,
>   and all the skye doth leane,
> There is the cave where Phebe layed,
>   the shepheard long to dreame.
>   (57–64)

The choice not to strive toward God is expressed in unimaginative a-
phorism: "To kerke the narre, from God more farre" (97). Propor-
tioning one's life to nature or proportioning one's art to nature means
seeing nature's patterns (high and low places in this case) in a way to
suggest a healthy variousness in man's life choices—a defiance of neat
systems and unequivocal moral dicta.

Just as Spenser gives good poetry to the hills he gives good poetry—
and thus a substantial argument—to the notion that contemporary life
has value, that nostalgia for the past may be simply unuseful. In "July,"
Spenser explores his contemporaries' relationship to the history of
man's fall from pristine simplicity. Life problems, one's social milieu,
temper the usefulness of the image of the golden world. Thomalin be-
haves (wrongly, perhaps) as though he is in an unfallen world. The
necessity for curative herbs for sick goats, which the mountains freely

provide, cannot be denied by reference to a past golden age when illness and corruption were not threats. Morrell's argument does make sense because it is not nature but man's relationship to it that has been corrupted. Our reading of the October eclogue tells us that Spenser has seized upon and felt the contingencies of historical circumstance; for him man must live face-to-face with his self-created circumstance. Although Spenser compares the relationship of Moses and other exemplary figures of the golden past to that of the Roman shepherds who "weltre in welths waves," the hill-dwelling Morrell troubles us by claiming "When folke bene fat, and riches rancke,/It is a signe of helth." Spenser recognizes that, just as nature herself provides a pattern to which man assigns value according to use, so material possessions gain negative value only in their misuse.[18] The choice is not between purity and contemporary corruption, but between deliberate poverty and simplicity that is antiprogressive, perhaps, in attitude and the rational use of worldly wealth.

Finally, the paradox of high versus low, striving versus humility, is most succinctly played out, in the last movement of the July eclogue, in the personal story of Algrind. After telling us that Algrind has acquiesced to a life of humility Spenser emphasizes, in the account of his choice, human and practical responses to historical circumstance rather than absolute responses to a "correct" theology. Spenser defies embracing any limiting system of moral choices that would condemn Algrind the good man or any good man. Clearly, Spenser's sympathies lie with Algrind—"a shepherd great in gree" who "sat upon a hyll"; he explains Algrind's having learned to love the low degree by describing hill life as simply imprudent and open to unpredictable dangers, but certainly not immoral. Algrind, who stands for Elizabeth's controversial archbishop, Grindal, had attempted to climb, for purest motives, to a distinctive position in the hierarchy of the Elizabethan church (discussed in detail in chapter 3). Spenser's approval of such ambition makes our reading of "July" one of open, argumentative inquiry.

The paradox of the fortunate fall may be a convenient expression of the problem of the July eclogue, but it also credits Spenser with a sharpness of mind that only emerges in other eclogues. He adopts Mantuan's high/low contrast, shows enough independence to invert it, but cannot quite manipulate the proportioning between man and nature to the extent that, for the sake of clarity, I have suggested he has. That is, the poem suggests that the figurative or moral reading of lowland living gives values to balance, unimpassioned simplicity, and freedom from danger. Highland living represents an enlightened Eve and Adam, vulnerable to despair and failure, but also having the possibility of exultation in the goodness of God. The loss of this possibility for the lowland dweller and its theological significance is never made explicit. Algrind teaches us "to love the lowe degree," but that is only because he was injured through climbing. Confusion reigns concerning the dwelling place of the saints—"The hylls where dwelled holy saints," but, also, "they . . . lived in lowlye leas." Spenser grapples with the problem but lacks the poetic precision and control to see it through in consistent pastoral rhetoric.

Variousness succeeds on a more personal level—the poem concludes with paradoxical emblems—Thomalin's is *In medio virtus* ("virtue dwellest in the middest"—E. K.) and Morrell's is *In Summo foelicitas* ("perfect felicity dwelleth in supremacie"—E. K.). These emblems confirm what Spenser had intended: from Mantuan's superficial contrast, he could build an experience of conflict combining both an observation of nature and a sense of a classical philosophical and moral problem. For once E. K. states it accurately and in theological terms: ". . . once I heard alleaged in defence of humilitye, out of a great doctour, 'Suorum Christus humillimus:' which saying a gentle man in the company taking at the rebownd, beate backe again with lyke saying of another doctoure, as he sayde, 'Suorum Deus altissimus.'"

v

Once we see that Spenser has freed pastoral from its Virgilian obligation to construct and question real geographical place and has found, instead, in Mantuan, a landscape based on Christian moral experience, the next phase in our search for the *Calender*'s sources takes us to the pastoral of Clément Marot. In imitating Marot, Spenser liberates pastoral from its allegorical limitation, and thus from its narrow character as a mode in which courtly figures wear country guise and speak with studied, highly charged simplicity.

Marot understands only remotely that, for Virgil, pastoral is an alternative world in which one examines one mode of life and art. In his pastorals, formulaic and stylized debate, not life choice, sets city against country, public against private, politics against nature. His fundamental experience of pastoral depends on his heritage of medieval allegory and his confident courtier's charm. Although the traditional pastoral inheritance of naiveté allows an unaccustomed boldness in addressing kings or other people in high places, and therefore depends upon qualities inherent in natural settings as opposed to those of courtly milieux, Marot assigns no values to the pastoral world beyond aesthetic or literary ones. Here his role as teacher of Spenser becomes critical, for, having elevated the decorative, aesthetic, courtly aspect of pastoral language at the expense of the ancient aspect (which explores the relationship between life choice and geographical place), he has laid the groundwork that would establish pastoral as a metaphoric, inclusive Spenserian language. In his own poetry, by use of allegory, Marot constructs parallel worlds of woods and court. He embellishes nature for two reason: first, to provide poetry attractive on its own merits; and, second to lend charm, a measure of the exotic, and even an ironic preciousness to the fully identifiable nonpastoral personae of the poem—in the case of Marot's *Eclogue III,* the figures Pan and Robin posing as François Ier and the poet himself.

The following discussion defines Marot's rigid allegorical mode and distinguishes it from Spenser's inclusive mode, which filters broad common life experiences through the language and conventions of pastoral. Marot assumes, from an exclusive court perspective, that pastoral guise has an enhancing effect on courtiers posing as rustics. The aristocrat, detached and unapproachable (even in his own milieu), becomes sympathetic, touching, and magical when, for example, he washes the poor man's feet. His landscape also takes on a double meaning. Marot's allegory has a transforming power that is similar to the meaning or force of an actual architectural French pastoral of some two centuries hence. In the renowned Petit Hameau at Versailles, a rustic farm designed for Marie Antoinette, wooden beams were painted on stone and the tiny yard could hold few animals, but it charmed by its childlike, precious aesthetic, which, of course, demanded comparison with the lavish grandeur of the chateau's formal gardens. The Hameau spoke of a reassuring simplicity and gentleness in royalty, of a kind of regal humility. Such humility, of course, depended on a pastoral convention that ignored the odor of barnyard and kitchen garden and idealized and tacitly praised the peasantry. The Hameau's roughness, a roughness too delicate for authentic French farmers and too crude for the Queen, brought peasant and noble together, and showed the best of both.

Such studied rusticity takes its language and descriptive material from classical pastoral but it denies the system of values from that natural, biological world. Its touchstones are royalty and court; its mode, intrigue—deciphering political or social events and identifying courtly actors. To Spenser goes the task of dissociating such pastoral from the *a clé* tradition and turning it into an independent, comprehensive moral language that establishes a commonality of experience between rustic and courtier.

If we compare a passage from Marot's "Pan et Robin" with Spenser's imitation of it in the December eclogue the two modes can be distinguished. Both poems begin in a *locus amoenus* in the mode of Virgil *II* or *VII*—"Ung pastoureau qui Robin s'appeloit,"[19] and "The gentle shepherd satte beside a spring,/All in the shadowe of a bushye brere." Marot's Robin begs that Pan deign to hear his *chansonettes champestres,* later emphasizing that he learned to play not, primarily, to win the contender's prize but, rather, to please Pan. (The analogy would be Virgil breaking the fiction of pastoral simplicity, saying explicitly that his object was to flatter his patron Maecenas and that he, as poet, stood beneath him in the social hierarchy—clearly a deferential tone that undercuts pastoral integrity.)[20] Spenser's Colin sings a "piteous mone" addressed to Pan, but is unashamedly introspective and analytical. His plaint addresses the world outside the pastoral landscape only indirectly, by having the singer proportion the pattern of his own unhappy love to any poet's or singer's archetypal, personal biography. Spenser, staying close to Marot, begins with youth in springtime. Here are *Pan et Robin* and the December eclogue:

> Sur le printemps de ma jeunesse folle,
> Je ressembloys l'arondelle qui volle
> Puis ça, puis là; l'aage me conduisoit,
> Sans peur ne soing, où le cueur me disoit.
> En la forest (sans la craincte des loups)
> Je m'en allois souvent cueillir le houx,
> Pour faire gluz à prendre oyseaulx ramaiges
> Tous differendz de chantz & de plumaiges;
> Ou me souloys (pour les prendre) entremettre
> A faire brics ou caiges pour les mettre;
> Ou transnouoys les riveieres profondes;
> Ou renforçoys sur le genoil les fondes; . . .
>   O quantes fois aux arbres grimpé j'ay,
> Pour denicher ou la pie ou le geay,
> Ou pour gecter des fruictz ja meurs & beaulx
> A mes compaings, qui tendoient leurs chappeaulx . . .
>   (15–32)

> 'Whilome in youth, when flowrd my joyfull spring,
> Like Swallow swift I wandered here and there:
> For heate of heedlesse lust me so did sting,
> That I of doubted daunger had no feare.
>   I went the wastefull woodes and forest wyde.
>   Withouten dreade of Wolves to bene espyed.

> I wont to raunge amydde the mazie thickette,
> And gather nuttes to make me Christmas game:
> And joyed oft to chace the trembling Pricket,
> Or hunt the hartlesse hare til shee were tame.
>   What recked I, of wintrye ages waste?
>   Tho deemed I, my spring would ever laste . . .

> Howe have I wearied, with many a stroke,
> The stately Walnut tree, the while the rest
>   Under the tree fell all for nuts at strife!
>   For unlike to me was libertee and lyfe.
>   (19–36)

Marot makes Robin a character in a pastoral setting who moves about the woods with childlike charm, decorative in his rustic milieu. Nature has its own, nonresonant, "closed" values, which do not impinge on or expand into the "outside" world. Picking holly, catching birds, swimming rivers, and tasting ripe fruit are not ways of talking about moral or philosophical problems through the language of nature—they simply describe literally what a child might do in the woods. Only knowing the allegorical key, knowing that Robin is the sophisticated courtier poet Marot, can the reader "translate" the poem into its second meaningful dimension of human nature: nature represents, in artificial pastoral guise, the period of youthfulness in the poet's life. It would be over-burdening the poem and giving its treatment of biological nature an inflated value to read "cueillir le houx," for example, as fraught with the same symbolic significance as "Yet once more, O ye laurels . . . I come to pluck your berries harsh and crude. . . ." Similarly, in Spenser, one cannot separate nature from her lessons, nor can one be free of a moral, value-assigning vision of the world as one could in Marot if the key were not known.

Some further comments about the passage above will dramatize the Spenserian continuity between nature and human nature. In the December eclogue, as in *Lycidas*, awareness of such continuity enriches but does not violate the poem. The phrases "when flowrd my joyfull spring" and "of wintrye ages waste" adeptly combine human "value" words (joyful, waste) with nature words (spring, winter) and, thus, as we have said earlier, accord life to the cycle of the seasons. Such phrases help the reader gauge, from one experience, the archetypal experience. Similarly, chasing the "trembling pricket" and hunting the "hartlesse hare til *shee* were tame" take on explicit dimensions that reflect the youthful, spring season of the speaker. "Hartlesse" and "trembling" move from animal qualities into the range of sexual, hesitant, tender human emotion. Finally, Spenser makes unambiguous and lucid his philosophical intent in the phrase "Tho deemed I, my spring would ever laste," and, again in the line that summarizes the description of shaking the stately (mature) walnut tree: ". . . Ylike to me was libertee and lyfe."

Marot has provided Spenser a skeleton, but Marot uses no such "value" adjectives, no summarizing phrases, to expand pastoral beyond the bounds of its landscape. Indeed, his inability to see such an option and the pressures to make the key known often push pastoral toward the brink of comedy.

In further examples in *Pan et Robin* and in Marot's *Elegie* for *Loyse de Savoye* (his first eclogue), the consequences of discontinuity between nature and human nature clearly result in a disquieting artificiality, both in character and in landscape. (Perhaps Johnson was right to complain of Milton that he never pastured flocks, but at least in *Lycidas* his lie was consistent.) A significant limitation in keeping separate nature and human nature is that one cannot then acknowledge consciously that the simple is only deceptively so, that rustic pastoral can express the complex. In *Pan et Robin* Marot would portray the psychological growth of an educated man, but the poet must find an indicator that reduces his character or landscape to pastoral size. We bridle when, having indentified the *bon Janot* as his father and teacher, Robin further affirms the authority of the elder's lessons by establishing a rural, formal tutorial hour, university style:

> Aussi le soir, que les trouppeaulx espars
> Estoient serrez & remis en leurs parcs,
> Le bon vieillart apres moy travailloit,
> Et a la lampe assez tard me veilloit . . .
> (61–64)

We are further jarred to find that the curriculum is the shepherd's handbook—Robin employs body and spirit to learn "a charpenter loges de boys portables/A les rouler de l'ung en l'autre lieu . . ./A eviter les dangereux herbages." The serious, court aspect of learning is at odds with the subject matter, which is founded, quite literally, on peasants' cultural requirements; nature's language proves limited in describing serious human endeavor. A figurative reading of such an *education sentimentale* in nature requires a more serious view of nature's patterns.

In the comparable education passage in Spenser's December eclogue the complexity of psychological and poetic growth finds rich, comprehensive expression in the vocabulary of nature. Note the grandeur and universality in Spenser's language, the poise that expands pastoral credibility just to its breaking point but not beyond:

> And tryed time yet taught me greater thinges:
> The sodain rysing of the raging seas,
> The soothe of byrds by beating of their wings,
> The power of herbs, both which can hurt and ease,
> And which be wont tenrage the restlesse sheepe,
> And which be wont to worke eternall sleepe.
>
> But ah, unwise and witlesse Colin Cloute!
> That kydst the hidden kinds of many a wede,
> Yet kydst not ene to cure thy sore hart roote . . .
> (85–93)

The stanza has an almost imperceptible movement from rustic landscape to Colin's hurtful love; it has, also, an incantatory structure that emphasizes and makes formal the repetitive aspect of learning and allows the reader to participate in the accumulation of experience; most important, such words as "sodain rysing," "raging," "power," "hurt," "ease," and "eternall sleep," set off by no palliating deflective detail, build a single, unified world that can admit of no translation. The poem creates all there is of Colin; he cannot unmask.

In Marot's *Elegie* for *Loyse de Savoye*[21] the one-dimensional pastoral landscape frequently clashes with character and exemplifies the tendency toward comedy. Aside from the obvious example of Loyse admonishing her young ladies-in-waiting to learn needlework even though their fathers are rich and powerful (*riche . . . et puissant*, ll. 67ff.), the royal, courtly values everywhere intrude. Even in the chorus Colin asserts:

Sus donc, mes Verse, chantez chants doloreux
Puis que la Mort a Loyse ravie
Qui tant tenoit *noz Courtilz* vigoreux . . .
(50–52)

And, later, Loyse's royal guidance is extolled; quasi-natural language defines her rôle—*le temps obscur, pluvieux*—but the words are not of the pastoral landscape, organic to the poem; they are merely a locution for trying historical circumstance:

Tant a de foys sa prudence monstreé
Contre *le temps obscur & pluvieux*,
Que France n'a (long temps a) recontree
Telle Bergere, au rapport des plus vieulx . . .
(149–152)

Loyse remains, always, a Marie Antoinette in the Hameau, a royal presence set off against an inappropriate landscape that serves both to idealize and simplify her, thus rendering her more attractive but also more inauthentic. William Empson gives us a rich definition of this; he calls it "the old pastoral." "The essential trick of the old pastoral, which was felt to imply a beautiful relation between rich and poor, was to make simple people express strong feelings (felt as the most universal subject, something fundamentally true about everybody) in learned and fashionable language (so that you wrote about the best subject in the best way). From seeing the two sorts of people combined like this you thought better of both; the best parts of both were used."[22] But it is this same pastoral, he maintains, that can become comic if the writer does not keep up "a firm pretence that he was unconscious of . . . [the clash between style and theme]. Such a pretence no doubt makes the characters unreal, but not the feelings expressed or even the situation described. . . ." Marot's failure to maintain a uniform pretense, his tendency to appear from "outside" as a young courtier, prevents our assent to a dual value system in which Loyse is both nymph and queen, her daughter both royal Marguerite and rustic "Margot d'excellence."

Finally, a comment on language, the element that separates the merely imitative poet in a tradition from the analytic, understanding one. A one-dimensional pastoral landscape, neither firm enough to "pastoralize" the royal figures in it nor expansive enough to allow them unhampered universal movement and expression, derives from a close, accurate imitation of the details of Virgilian pastoral landscape; significantly, it is an imitation lacking the larger classical context. Marot may describe landscape—flora and fauna—in detail. The passage above from *Pan et Robin* cites specific species of birds, just as Virgil might name herbs—*L'arondelle, la pie, le geay*; it claims an interest in bird-watching and differentiating songs and plumage and describes making cages to contain captured birds. As long as Marot's context is courtly such details, though decorative, are irrelevant. If a Virgilian figure trapped birds the act would indicate—fantasy-like—imprisonment of pastoral song. For Marot meaning must come from outside the pastoral world, for his characters neither live there (as Virgil's do) nor take their self-definition and life patterns from nature; his nature does not have this resonance, but is more the mode of an occasional, holiday *déjeuner sur l'herbe*.

Marot constructs imitations of real geographical places but does not believe in them as alternatives. (As a curious, civilized man, he might investigate rural communes and briefly play the requisite rôle, but his urban context would forbid him to establish permanent residence.) Spenser, on the other hand, ignores imitation of Virgilian detail or its mirror in Marot unless it expands into moral, evaluative terms the pastoral experience. To Marot's phrase—I resembled the lark that flew here and there—Spenser adds, "For heate of heedlesse lust me so did sting,/ That I of doubted daunger had no feare." This phrase accentuates the universal fearlessness and sexual energy of youth and leads to an embellishment of Marot's assertion that he went about the forest without fear of wolves. Thus Spenser's lack of fear of the wasteful woods calls up an understood, psychological restlessness that accompanies youth's first erotic sensations. Such a comment on language merely supports the notion, discussed earlier in the chapter, that Spenser takes on Virgilian ideas (love, death, the craft of poetry), and that he ignores an exclusively biological nature, and its precise, technical vocabulary. This is what I mean by his analytic understanding.

We asked at the outset what changes occurred in the pastoral idea as it moved from Virgil to Spenser. In particular, we asked if the content and value of pastoral landscape changed. We took as poles Virgil's vision of the pastoral world and private life in nature (which was representative of one alternative for man) and Spenser's vision of the life of man proportioned after the patterns of nature. We attempted to explain the discrepancy between the sixteenth-century reader's view of Virgil and Mantuan as pastoral twins and the twentieth-century reader's obliviousness to Mantuan in terms of the demands that Spenser, as an ideal Renaissance reader, would have made upon poetry. Spenser, we concluded, found Mantuan's attraction in his secure Christian moralizing—his confident use of pastoral convention in the perspective of ethical behavoir—and not in his particular, eclectic, unsystematic pastoral landscape or in his ability to see the richness in the pastoral idea itself.

Mantuan's eclogues are not sufficiently clear in conception to have taken seriously the Virgilian questions of life in nature or to have presented a coherent allegorical pastoral. Marot provides allegory for Spenser, who, we discovered, has made a decision that his own personal powers and historical circumstance make pastoral his appropriate mode. Allegory demands from Marot a ficitional "real" landscape; adapted by Spenser it becomes his single mode of expression in *The Shepheardes Calender*. In *The Calender* he asks his reader to experience a variety of common human emotions. Unlike his pastoral predecessors, who either rejected the mode for its limitations (as Virgil did) or expanded it to the point of unpoetic artificiality (as Marot did), Spenser can speak in it and move his readers.

In *An Apologie for Poetrie* Sir Philip Sidney, following Horace, declares, "Moving is of a higher degree than teaching."[23] Spenser's best work depends on moving the reader toward reasoned virtue, as do the works of Milton, Marvell, and Herbert—the most significant of Spenser's pastoral successors. Sidney goes on to remark that the poet is monarch: "For he dooth not only show the way, but giveth so sweete a prospect into the way, as will intice any man to enter it. . . . He beginneth not with obscure definitions, which must blur the margent with interpretations . . . but he commeth to you with words set in delightefull proportion."[24] The choice to sing in pastoral voice, to avoid the mystification of allegory, and to make manifest universally accessible patterns in nature makes Spenser an enticing poet by Sidney's measure—a poet who exhibits by his will to make experience accessible and understood a deep and abiding loyalty to all that is human.

CHAPTER 2

The Calender's Pastoral Rhetorics:
"Formall Roomes in Wexen Frame"

In the December eclogue Colin portrays the summer season of his life as a time when he was "wont to seeke the honey Bee,/ Working her formall roomes in Wexen frame" (67-68). This phrase well describes the intricate play between *The Calender*'s ordered verse and its flexible, imaginative use of pastoral expression.[1] Indeed, Spenser's ability to extend or expand pastoral speech so that the reader is led to participate in the world inside the poem is, I believe, the central experience of the most successful poems of the cycle *and* the experience that has most frequently baffled critics of the poem. Attuned to pastoral as either a kind of decorative poetry or as a kind of witty puzzle requiring a key to its allegory, modern readers resist Spenser's invitation to grieve, to celebrate, and to question commonplace human experience in a language drawn from nature. Hallett Smith is quite correct when he asserts, concerning criticism of *The Calender*, "Covert allusion to contemporary persons and events have been so laboriously and painfully investigated that it is with some difficulty that a modern reader threads his way through all the apparatus that has been provided for the poetry to the poetry itself."[2] What I am after is "the poetry itself," the meaning drawn from the poise between formality and flexibility, and, in this chapter particularly, Spenser's ability to transform the conventions of pastoral into what I call a "variety of pastoral rhetorics." These rhetorics include simple, rustic, English pastoral; elaborate, mythological pastoral; social, countryside pastoral; and, in the April eclogue, Christian pastoral; these pastoral rhetorics, mingled, contrasted, or used singly, compose the techniques by which Spenser expands the pastoral world.

In Chapter 1, I traced the evolution of Spenser's pastoral idea as it defined man's relationship to nature and the poetry of nature—pastoral. My focus was on Spenser as a reader and creator of pastoral. By analyzing his relationship to an ancient source (Virgil) and to two contemporary sources (Mantuan and Marot), I concluded that, as a critical

42

Renaissance reader, Spenser took a decisive step that severed English
pastoral at the outset of its most productive period from narrow imita-
tion of earlier pastoral poets. Spenser, as yet untroubled by the physical
and social realities of peasant life, at home with the "artificiality" of
the mode, created a pastoral free from its ties to geographical place and
from its reliance on allegorical narrative.

Chapter 2, a "reading" of selected eclogues from *The Calender*,
depends on neither the evolution of an idea nor the reconstruction
of the Renaissance mind. It proceeds on the assumption that, because
Spenser is concerned with the conventional, the commonplace, and,
thus, with ordinary human responses to the world, his pastoral should
move serious readers of poetry today. Thus I test a truism that might
have pleased Spenser—poetry is a universal language. The dialogue
in chapter 2 is between Spenser and us. I believe that Spenser provides,
not an argument for a specific view of human nature, but an experience,
for his reader, of a human nature that he had begun to define even early
in his career.

The chapter begins with a close reading of the January eclogue in
order to treat problems of and approaches to Spenser's pastoral rheto-
rics (which are later examined in detail). The analysis of "January"
defines the reader's relation to narrator and pastoral characters, the
moral, metaphoric use of nature's landscape, and the technique of ex-
ploiting fully pastoral convention. Section iii focuses on Spenser's tech-
nique in the November elegy for expanding the conventions of pastoral
death to include all death. In sections iv and v Spenser's varied rhetorics
are sorted out and analyzed as they appear in the confusing June and
quintessential April eclogues.

ii

The skeletal narrative of "January" is quite simple. Colin Clout,
Spenser's persona or pastoral mask in *The Calender*, appears in a winter
landscape, he and his sheep wan and pale. He beseeches the gods of love
to pity him and says that he visualizes the January landscape as a mirror
of his plight. Rosalind reproves him and his singing; thus neither his
Muse nor his pipe give him comfort. Finally he breaks his oaten pipe in
disgust. The arrival of an evening in keeping with his "pensife" mood
sends him homeward.

Despite the simplicity of the narrative, the first stanzas of "January"
reveal, in their complexity, the terms of *The Calender*'s poetic world.

> A shepeheards boye (no better doe him call)
> When Winters wastful spight was almost spent,
> All in a sunneshine day, as did befall,

Led forth his flock, that had bene long ypent.
So faynt they woxe, and feeble in the folde,
That now unnethes their feete could them uphold.
All as the Sheepe, such was the shepeheards looke,
For pale and wanne he was, (alas the while,)
May seeme he lovd, or els some care he tooke:
Well couth he tune his pipe, and frame his stile.

(1-10)

Indeed, the first line of the eclogue is surprising. We read three words
and are stopped abruptly by a parenthetical address to us, the readers.
Furthermore, the narrator of these remarks makes certain assumptions
about us—that we are better than his pastoral character, that we may
try to transform the shepherd into one worthy of us. However, as we
read on, the boy's poetry and his person become attractive to us. We
feel pleasingly humble in responding to him as if we were equals. It is
not long before we wish ourselves as good as shepherds, as much in
touch with nature, as full of special value. In the parenthetical phrases
and other addresses to the reader, Spenser employs the central power of
pastoral, what is, perhaps, its hallmark. In William Empson's view the
mode is "based on a double attitude of the artist to the worker, or the
complex man to the simple one (I am in one way better, in another not
so good), and this may well recognize a permanent truth about the
aesthetic situation."[3]

A peculiarity of Spenser's pastoral also appears in the opening lines.
Although drawn to the shepherd's boy initially, we must recognize that
his story is insignificant by comparison with the evaluative language
that surrounds it. In the first four lines, the story goes, a boy led his
flock. Meaning rests in the evaluative and qualifying language that sets
sunshine against winter's wasteful spite and defines generalized human
frailty in the words "faint," "feeble," "pale," "wan," "spent," and
"ypent." For Spenser single characters are merely convenient vehicles
for expressing emblematic human moods and circumstances.

The opening lines of the eclogue establish still another hallmark of
Spenser's pastoral. Point of view is never self-consciously complicated
by discrepancies between poet, narrator, and characters or by the use of
a critical voice within the poem that challenges the poem's very terms.
The narrator never tricks us; indeed, in line nine, he is as much in the
dark as we—"May seeme he lovd, or els some care he tooke." He simp-
ly reassures us that, if we listen with him, we will discover the source
of woe. The narrator and the reader have one vantage point and become,
in effect, one figure. They create the verse, listen to it, and believe it
because it describes the whole world. Spenser acknowledges no sophisti-
cated, critical perspective outside of the pastoral world.

Colin's lack of dimension as a real character would only become a problem if the poet's mode were not ingenuous naiveté but the more complex irony of seventeenth-century verse. In Donne's "The Extasie" the lovers' dialogue changes its meaning as we take into account the varied positions of the potential commentators. Both hypothetical voyeur who stands "within convenient distance" and the lover who hears "this dialogue of one" at the end of the poem are creations of the imagination of the speaker and provide him a vehicle by which he can stand at a distance from himself and his belovèd, who form together supposedly "a single, pure soul." Thus the reader, like the speaker, must attempt to reconcile or make precise the irony of the situation by stepping even further back; he cannot accept the speaker's literal description of himself, his love, or the hypothetical comments of the intruding others, because the various voices conflict. One issue for example—the necessity to release the body from prison—is invalid if the souls' mingling has been wholly satisfying.

In Spenser's work such complication of point of view would be the poet's failure, not his intention. This is, indeed, exactly the problem of Spenser's late pastoral eclogue "Colin Clout's Come Home Againe." In *The Shepheardes Calender* Spenser provides guidance for us when there are two conflicting sets of evaluative terms, such as the rustic and royal ones in "April." He shows us that these do not shatter the pastoral world by exploding its fiction; rather, they deepen its significance from within.

Having defined the reader's relationship to the verse, it is possible now to ask what meanings the surfaces of the poem yield. In Colin's monologue "Ye Gods of love," which begins at line 13 and takes up ten of the poem's thirteen stanzas, the singer addresses just the issues the narrator guessed he would, as well as the central issues of pastoral: "May seeme he *lovd*, or els some *care* he tooke:/Well couth he *tune his pipe*, and *frame his stile*" (9–10) (emphasis added). However, his mode of speech may surprise the reader. We expect Colin's troubled state of mind and its pictorial representation in the natural landscape to be drawn out to show how winter's barrenness mirrors or is like disappointed love. We expect a series of analogies that will preserve the integrity and separateness of human and natural worlds. Conceivably, we might anticipate the convention called "pathetic fallacy," in which streams would cease to flow and flowers to bloom in sympathy with the pastoral mourner. However, we can make no such precise analogies in Spenser's world. Human nature and the nature of conventional seasonal description are entwined in an original and even startling fashion in order to explicate the psychological and moral qualities of love pain. Nature loses its material referent, and becomes a language. (Nature's language "explains" the *Calender*'s world, for example, in the way Marxist or psychoanalytical language might explain today's world.) Paul Alpers calls this technique "the rhetorical use of pictorial description."[4] An analogy that does not make pictorial sense turns out to be a skillful and deliberate metaphor for the change and disorder that characterize Colin's love. Furthermore, meaning does not derive from what Colin sees but from what he thinks and feels *when* he sees, as in the following stanzas:

> Thou barrein ground, whome winters wrath hath wasted,
> Art made a myrrhour, to behold my plight;
> Whilome thy fresh spring flowrd, and after hasted
> Thy sommer prowde with Daffadillies dight.
> And now is come thy wynters stormy state,
> Thy mantle mard, wherein thou maskedst late.
>
> (19-24)

> Such rage as winters, reigneth in my heart,
> My life blood friesing with unkindly cold;
> Such stormy stoures do breede my balefull smart,
> As if my yeare were wast, and woxen old.
> And yet alas, but now my spring begonne,
> And yet alas, yt is already donne.
>
> (25-30)

Although winter's barren ground is called a "mirror," what Colin beholds is not a realistic image but an evaluative metaphor given meaning by the responsive poet's mind. Winter touches off a reflective process in the lover, who immediately forgets the season, and daydreams about the springtime of his love. By the time Spenser returns to winter landscape with its marred mantle, he has entwined nature and human nature to such an extent that no truly visual quality or precise analogy remains. We note, for example, that the analogy "such rage as winters" is paralleled, two lines later, by "such stormy stoures" (tumult, conflict), but the "as" has been dropped, so comparison with winter season recedes. The storms are human.

The second stanza uses nature to depict the process of change. This use of seasonal change confirms my point that Spenser sees simultaneity between patterns in nature and patterns in man's experience. By exploiting the inevitable processes of natural change—trees losing their leaves, seasonal cycles—Spenser represents timely transformation worked on the mind of man by his emotional experience. The two stanzas enforce change by verbs and adverbs that counterpose times against each other: "whilome . . . and after hasted" (21), and "now my spring begonne,/ . . . yt is already donne" (29-30). The flowers, summer daffodils, are there because this is pastoral—Spenser has been taken to task for not knowing or, more likely, not caring that daffodils are the spring flower *par excellence*[5] —but what carries weight is that human feelings of freshness and pride change to barrenness and sterility.

Spenser's vocabulary is always moral and judgmental rather than objective or descriptive. Such words as "barrein," "wrath," "stormy," "mard," "stoures," "unkindly," "cold," and "balefull" are chosen by the *mind*, not the *eye*, of the observer. Even where there is a clear etymological connection between figurative (moral) meaning and visual phenomena, Spenser chooses to use nature's language rhetorically and morally. For example, the word "waste" in the eclogue occurs twice to qualify winter and twice to describe Colin: "Winters wastful spight" (2), "winters wrath hath wasted" (19), "as if my yeare were wast," (28), "my buds . . . are wasted" (38). "Waste" becomes a chorused word in the eclogue cycle, occurring in every poem except the festive awakening poems of "March" and "April." In the word "waste," Spenser could bring together and emphasize its two meanings: first, "objective, descriptive"—"waste" has its root in Latin *vastus*, meaning "a desert land" —and, second, "subjective, judgmental"—"waste" means to perform no useful function, to expend needlessly.[6] But, for Spenser, the desert waste is always a metaphor for emptiness. The neutral, geographical landscape does not interest him.

In the January eclogue there are two clear echoes of Virgil's *Eclogues I* and *II*, appropriate as Spenser begins his eclogue cycle and useful in distinguishing Spenser's pastoral world from Virgil's. Late in his plaint, Colin hints at the narrative events that produced his care and pain. He had encountered a certain fair "shee" in "the neighbour towne." He says, "A thousand sithes I curse that carefull hower,/Wherein I longd the neighbour towne to see . . . " (48-49). The convention is central to pastoral; it compares the complex place to the simple one, the city to the country, and is a foil for heightening the naiveté of the rustic singer. Virgil renders it differently in *Eclogue II*.

> Urbem, quam dicunt Romam, Meliboee putavi
> stultus ego huic nostrae similem.
>
> (18-19)

(Naive as I was, I fancied, Melibe,/This city they call Rome was much like ours.)

Virgil's comparison gives reality to the rural world; the shepherd makes informed choices and lives in a world that can go on without poetry. Landscape has its own echoing voice—cicadas chirp in the bushes; mountains, rocks and groves resound; and the singer lifts his voice to a responsive landscape.[7] Spenser's nature is imaginary and can appear and disappear. Rosalind's town suddenly appears, not to define or compare places, but to express the true joy and pain of love. City-country comparison is irrelevant to *The Calender*. The country world is the only world, and its reality or unreality go unquestioned. The second echo, however, shows Spenser's interest in Virgil's depiction of love. The Amaryllis, Corydon, Alexis relationships of Virgil, *Eclogue II*, parallel the January pattern—Hobbinol loves Colin, who loves Rosalind.[8]

For Virgil, nature's own attractiveness (or poetry about it) builds and defines character. No mediating, evaluative vocabulary is necessary. The Corydon of Virgil's second eclogue is his landscape; his vision of himself depends upon his place in nature:

> despectus tibi sum, nec qui sim quaeris, Alexi,
> quam dives pecoris, nivei quam lactis abundans.
> (19–20)

> (I am unlovely to you, nor do you ask who I am, Alexis, how rich in livestock, how overflowing with snowy milk.)

The *qui sim* (who I am) *is* keeper of rich flocks, *is* producer of overflowing white milk, is the dark berry (*vaccinia nigra*) of a few lines earlier. Corydon's melancholy, his burning in love (*urere*), and his lack of success move us because his compelling natural gifts, offered to Alexis, are one with our attraction for nature and poetry. Spenser's Hobbinol also gives gifts, but they are only tokens of conventional love, the manners of courtship, and are clearly separate from Hobbinol; they are not his identity.

> It is not Hobbinol, wherefore I plaine;
> Albee my love he seeke with dayly suit:
> His clownish gifts and curtsies I disdaine,
> His kiddes, his cracknelles, and his early fruit.
> Ah, foolish Hobbinol, thy gyfts bene vayne:
> Colin them gives to Rosalind againe.
> (55–60)

In Spenser, emphasis falls not on nature's gifts but, rather, on the pattern of rejections—the complaining, seeking, and giving again. Our attraction is to a pattern of rhetoric that sounds the melancholy chords of human distress in love.

A second illuminating echo of Virgil's *nec qui sim* . . . distinguishes between Virgil's use of nature as definition and the typical Renaissance use of nature as decoration—stylized, conventional, and not weighted by moral problems. This distinction is particularly important for the pastoral lyric. In Sir Philip Sidney's early entertainment *The Lady of May*,[9]

nature ornaments, pays a courtly compliment. The shepherd woos the
May lady:

> Two thousand sheepe I have as white as milke,
> Though not so white as is thy lovely face.[10]

Nature defines at two removes; the speaking voice evaluates the pastoral
aesthetic (as white as milk, or, in another mode as white as snow—
phrases praising purity, virginity) and then makes the aesthetic into a
language of praise separate from nature. If Sidney derives poetic energy
from a real nature, the source of that energy lies far beneath the surface
of his figurative language. In the pastoral of the '80s and '90s and later,
poets like Sidney have access to a "frozen" literary world. Sidney can
use pastoral easily as a mode of social discourse because the reader's
familiarity with convention frees him from the burden of explanation.
We, as readers, recognize immediately that the phrase "two thousand
sheep as white as milk" means "extravagant beauty," not "flocks as far
as the eye can see." Further, the phrase does this with the duality that
is the hallmark of pastoral—flattery wearing the guise of simplicity; the
reader responds to flattery, not to livestock.

The Shepheardes Calender, too, uses pastoral as a form of social dis-
course, but what disconcerts both Renaissance and contemporary readers
of Spenser is that Spenser continually behaves as though each "frozen"
convention has an origin that must be explored; rather than borrow
fixed phrases he expands them with a seemingly unselfconscious intelli-
gence. At the end of the January eclogue, for example, Colin Clout de-
stroys his pastoral instrument: "So broke his oaten pype, and downe
dyd lye" (72). Some critics have been troubled by this act, failing to
recognize that it is a complex example of the mode's power as social
discourse and not an inappropriate comment on the limitation and pos-
sibility of pastoral song. Virgil proves, as always, the right point of
departure, although he and Spenser differ on the questions of limits and
range of emotion that each is capable of expressing in pastoral.

Virgil constantly tests the limits of pastoral, asking what themes,
what human emotions, what landscapes remain within the boundaries
of its expressive capabilities. A cartographer's chart of the limits of the
pastoral world has meaning in Virgil's eclogues and is even responsible
for our discomfort at the perhaps politically expedient hint that non-
pastoral Rome protects the existence of the pastoral world. Indeed, in
Eclogue IX geographical boundaries set out in *Eclogue I* are reiterated:

> certe equidem audieram, qua se subducere colles
> incipiunt mollique iugum demittere clivo,

usque ad aquam et veteres, iam fracta cacumina, fagos
omnia carminibus vestrum servasse Menalcan.

(7–10)

(But as I heard, from where our hills begin / To rise, and where their ridge slopes
gently down / To the stream's beeches with their doddered tops—/ Hadn't Menal-
cas saved it all through song?)

But the syntactically fragmented phrase—*veteres, iam fracta cacumina,*
fagos—suggest that the domain of pastoral song has already been threat-
ened, invaded by strangers (*advenae*). These outsiders, like alien literary
modes or nonpastoral places (Rome), cannot be accommodated in the
locus amoenus.

In *Eclogue II* the safety of the pastoral world is signaled by the
thick beeches, which give a protective shade (*densas, umbrosa cacumina,*
fagos); now these shade-giving treetops (*cacumina*) are broken along with
an *otium*, which is a pipe dream of the past. *Eclogue X* confirms the in-
trusion of nonpastoral reality. The poet Gallus is also a soldier, so social
and political realities color his biography and turn his songs toward epic.
Pastoral can neither keep him from death (the doom of disappointed
love) nor celebrate his departure appropriately. For Virgil, who follows
Theocritus quite self-consciously in this matter, there are uniquely pas-
toral ideas, limited in their appropriateness for expressing human exper-
ience.

Spenser simply *assumes* the mode's reality. No map can locate Rosa-
lind's town; it exists because there are towns in a literary rural commun-
ity, just as there are "cracknelles" (a kind of biscuit) but no pastries.
These marks authenticate the mode and their spontaneous generation
allows the reader an unlimited supply of pastoral touchstones, a world
of literary convention. If private life in nature yields no fruitful love in
Virgil's pastoral, in epic or heroic verse love may be born. For Spenser,
change of mode alters only the vocabulary of human emotion, not the
quality of human experience. There is love in Spenser's world, and pas-
toral or heroic verse can express it. Colin's broken pipe does not chal-
lenge the pastoral idea, not does it signal an end to poetry—that would
be curious at the beginning of an eclogue cycle—rather, it stands simply
as a radical but still conventional expression of the end of a dramatic
performance of pastoral despair.

Even when, in the October eclogue, Spenser confronts the tradition-
al temptation to turn to epic or tragic writing, he wants, primarily, to
shift rhetorical gears—he "thinks to throwe out thondring words of
threate" (104). Spenser asks not what he can perform in pastoral, but
whether he has done it as pastoral demands. I do not mean to suggest
that Spenser thinks he can write an epic of heroic deeds in pastoral, but,

rather, that his reading of historical and personal contingencies tell him that such an attempt is out of bounds for any poet contemporary with him. Virgil asserts the opposite; he may not be ready to write epic (as *Eclogues VI* and *VIII* demonstrate) but historical circumstance makes the time right for other poets' epics.

The January eclogue exemplifies the use of two particularly characteristic rhetorical techniques that expand the pastoral mode. First, the poet repeats and reforms certain figures, but in particularly precise and dense poetic language. Second, he expands to fullness conventions in the mainstream of the tradition. Two examples of the first technique are:

> Ye Gods of love, that pitie lovers payne,
> (If any gods the paine of lovers pitie:)
> (12–13)

> I love thilke lasse, (alas why doe I love?)
> And am forlorne, (alas why am I lorne?)
> (60–61)

The figures work by making an assertion—"I love thilke lasse," then the word order is rearranged, turning the assertion to question itself. The gods do pity lovers in pastoral but, just as conventionally, the lover doubts if the gods pity him at all. By so tightly juxtaposing contradictory stances, Spenser encloses the range of emotion between sympathetic pity and cold neglect. By questioning within the poem the very assumptions upon which convention rests, the poet closes in the pastoral world and shuts off disbelief.

In the December eclogue a formal rhetorical pattern succinctly presents two sides of an unextraordinary convention—that of the fatal love wound. Colin, the sole speaker in the final eclogue, asks himself a rhetorical question appropriate to the melancholy mood of the harvest season of his life:

> Why livest thou stil, and yet hast thy deathes wound?
> Why dyest thou stil, and yet alive art founde?
> (95–96)

Either question renders the convention adequately, and each alone is a hyperbolic expression of love pain. Taken together, however, the questions confirm Spenser's interest in the pattern of contradiction itself, the ambiguity of feeling that love engenders by denying life and simultaneously sustaining it. Life moves toward death, then death moves toward life. Enclosed in the movement is the emotional range of love and the subject of poetry. The formal rhetorical figures expand and contract and, ultimately, guide the reader's expectations toward an affirmation of life.

With the breaking of the pipe in "January," Colin ends his plaint. The closing frame exemplifies "full" convention, harmonious poetry in the mainstream of the tradition. Hallett Smith suggests that the conclusion of the January eclogue be compared with *Lycidas*. Milton, he says, shifts from a "tone of austere rejoicing . . . to the pastoral environment and level of feeling. . . . There is something more here than the mere close of the pastoral elegy."[11] To the contrary, this *is* the conventional formal close to a traditional eclogue—not an exultation in grief, but a continuation of the mood of melancholy into an emblematic nature:

> By that, the welked Phoebus gan availe,
> His weary waine, and nowe the frosty Night
> Her mantle black through heaven gan overhaile.
> Which seene, the pensife boy halfe in despight
> Arose, and homeward drove his sonned sheepe,
> Whose hanging heads did seeme his carefull case to weepe.
>
> (73–78)

In Colin's now-familiar vocabulary of grief—weary, frosty, pensive, careful—winter landscape takes on its human value, while the level of visual reality rises. Independent of Colin, Spenser affirms the proportion between man and nature. The poem has defined a conventional pattern of experience and thought that is confirmed in the conventional pattern of nature just at the moment when Colin seems to have "broken" pastoral possibility. "Phoebus gan availe . . . Night . . . gan overhaile"—these phrases describe the cycle of nature and affirm life, as do the rhetorical figures. They set us at a distance from Colin because, ultimately, the linear flow of human life is less capricious and more dependable than he is. Nature intrudes, not to end song, but to establish a ritual of order and poetic harmony.

These lines are the fullest rendering of the convention—nightfall/poem's end—in *The Calender*. "June" has four "homeward" lines. "June," "February," "March," "April," "May," "August," and "November" use the word "home" or "homeward" in their final verses. These words are a kind of shorthand for signaling the conventional termination of the poems, the harmony between nature (here the cycle of day and night) and human activity. In Virgil's second eclogue the hours of the day can be marked in the verse from noon to the time of doubled shadows. Spenser's poem has no diurnal course. Spenser does not fear that shadows hurt singers. Human behavior, human experience, and a distinctly human visualization and interpretaion of nature define Spenser's pastoral garment.

In this analysis of the January eclogue I have indicated the issues that arise when the reader of Spenser trusts his verse and allows its power to move him. He must place himself in relation to poet, narrator, and characters. He must trust the surface of the verse, although surfaces may indicate that anticipated visual, pictorial, reality has given way to "the rhetorical use of pictorial diction." Spenser, in effect, creates his own pastoral language, in which the reader responds to rhetorical patterns taken from human experience and confirmed and articulated through the vocabulary of nature. In "January" we perceived that there were no uniquely pastoral issues but, rather, a pastoral language that, in this first small poem, could be opened and given play and scope. In the following pages of the chapter I develop our understanding of these issues by analyzing the November, June, and April eclogues, which illustrate the development of Spenser's rhetoric or language and its effect on the reader.

iii

The November eclogue, an elegy for an unidentified Dido, uses poetic experience to reconcile us with death. Death, as Horace tells us, beats equally at every door. Dido's death, like the great but puzzling moment of Amoret's torture in *The Faerie Queene* (Book III), expresses representative human—not individual or singular—love and suffering—not only pastoral death, but our death as well. Another side of Spenser's pastoral inclusiveness, then, is his concern for the human effect of poetry on the reader. This reading of "November" specifies the poetic techniques by which Spenser includes his reader in understanding and, ultimately, acknowledging mortality.

"November" has even less of a skeletal narrative than "January" does. Thenot and Colin discuss possible songs to be sung and decide that a song of "deathes dreeriment" accords best with "season chill." Thenot values singing skill and promises Colin "greater gyfts" if he can equal in quality his plaints for Rosalind. Colin abruptly summons Melpomene, Muse of tragedy, and the Kentish shepherds to mourn in "carefull verse" (with the double meaning, "full of care"), the death of the shepherd's daughter Dido. In accord with convention the singer questions the continuation of his own life and the paradoxical life, death, and rebirth of flowers. Of Dido we learn merely that she existed in the same social world as Rosalind—that of curds, cracknels, and "clouted" cream—and that she represented paradigmatic beauty and humility. For her, nature's kindly course is "undon"; floods gasp, flocks refuse food. In a transitional passage, Colin registers the trustlessness of earthly things, then turns his verse to a joyful celebration of Dido's place as goddess in blissful Elisian fields. Thenot presents Colin with a cosset—a lamb brought up without a dam, according to E. K. With this appropriately sad gift presented and rain beginning to fall around them, the two shepherds depart homeward.

Although the November elegy for Dido imitates more directly and consistently the totality of a single poem than any other eclogue in Spenser's cycle, it varies profoundly from its model, Marot's elegy for Loyse de Savoye, and from the model pastoral elegy, Virgil's fifth eclogue. Unlike that of Marot's poem, this poem's power depends not on the graceful assembling of literary conventions, but on the philosophical exploration of conventions' origin in archetypal human experience. Spenser, here at his imposing best, moves vertically, combining patterns of nature and of human behavior, and horizontally, from the genre pastoral to collective human experience.

Virgil's *Eclogue V* has an impenetrable and schematized perfection in which balance, symmetry, and order convince us of the transformation of emotion for death from sorrow to glory. The poem excludes, narrows its choice of poetic experience, and limits itself to the pastoral way of death, the quality of which is "lower" than heroic death in emotional range and poetic expression. Marot's poem also excludes by its aristocratic moral certitude; the pastoral mode expresses in felicitous rhetoric what is already known—that royal Loyse ornaments Elisium. Individualizing details of Loyse's courtly life and death cause breaks in the pastoral fabric, and, although they are explained by the exigency of the allegory, these breaks further prevent the reader from identifying his experience with Loyse's. The poem's components—rustic and courtly worlds—tend to separate, to resist the building of integrated values, and, above both worlds, Loyse presides.

Virgil's opening lines do not inform us that death is the subject of the song that follows:

Cur non, Mopse, boni quoniam convenimus ambo,
tu calamos inflare leves, ego dicere versus
his corylis mixtas inter consedimus ulmos?
(1–3)

(Mopsus, why not, since we are both good men, / You with a Pan's pipe, I at making verse, / Sit here among the hazelwoods and elms?)

Like Theocritus' *Eclogue I*, Virgil's pastoral struggle with death can be labeled an exercise in song; it is repeatedly called *carmina* and then a subgenre of *carmina*, one among other species—*ignes, laudes,* and *iurgia*. Further, the frame with its elms, hazels, and beeches, its light breezes, inviting caves, and available sheepsitters, is a benign and protective environment where the central pastoral occupations of piping and singing seem an appropriate extension of the landscape. Even contention between singers lacks, Mopsus yielding gracefully—*tu maior*—just as Amyntas yields to Menalcas or pale olive to supple willow. This is pastoral *comme il faut*.

This poem, at the center of Virgil's cycle, is most profoundly within the pastoral world of *otium*, where even death can be accommodated. Daphnis establishes a kind of rapprochement between shepherds and gods and, through his apotheosis, makes human pastoral values eternal. For Mopsus' startling first word of elegy, "*exstinctum*," there is the redeeming first word, "*candidus*," of Menalcas' final speech. Phillip Damon, in his chapter on Virgilian pastoral, must have this sense of *V* when he calls the *sepulchrum Bianoris* of *Eclogue IX* "the Eclogue's first mention of death as a physical fact."[12] Daphnis' death is exclusively a pastoral death, and is unlike that signified by the tomb of *Eclogue IX*. Daphnis' death can be counted as only a very limited and special pastoral case. Damon illuminates the exclusive and fragile shell that shields Daphnis in contrast to figures in *Eclogues IX* and *X*: "Moeris' 'omnia fert aetas' and Gallus' 'omnia vincit amor' both admit an imperative larger than pastoral *otium*. They introduce the emotional and political reality which Arcadia cannot stand very much of."[13] In other words, Virgil undercuts his own vertical, integrated world of nature by allowing the intrusion of a parallel, previously excluded, political and philosophical world.

The botanical aspect of Virgil's landscape—its carefully differentiated plants, its natural and unnatural growth—is the primary source of meaning in the eclogue; death occurs in a preexisting pastoral world. For Marot, on the other hand, the death of an important individual precedes the poem, changing the poet's commitment to pastoral; that is, the philosophical question is no longer how pastoral values can accommodate death, but, much more superficially, how pastoral machinery (convention) is used to write elegy and eulogy. Because there is a nature in Virgil, Dr. Johnson would never have questioned Daphnis being more beautiful than his sheep, but he would have laughed at the picture of the royal Loyse teaching needlepoint and husbandry to the *jeunes Bergères* of France.[14] Dr. Johnson would claim that Marot's ornamental pastoral is artificial because there is no integral landscape, no limited, physical world. Marot's pastoral, as we saw in chapter 1, is a kind of allegorical rhetoric in which we must balance two worlds—that of *jeunes Bergères*, and that of the nobility; the latter translates pastoral into appropriately royal and aristocratic terms.

The frame of Marot's eclogue illustrates the absence of physical nature. While the opening lines respond to Theocritian and Virgilian *loci,* this landscape is only an imitation of a literary *place*:

En ce beau Val sont plaisirs excellens,
  Ung cler Ruisseau bruiant pres de l'ombrage,
  L'herbe a soubhait, les vents non violens,
  Puis toy, Colin, qui de chanter faiz rage.
                    (1-4)

The *beau val, cler ruisseau, ombrage, herbe,* and *vents* have no geogra-
phy, not even in a map of the mind. In ancient pastoral, shepherds choose
a place, sit down in it, walk to it—*succesimus antro, succedimus antro,
consedimus hic*—and thereby lend presence to their world, mapping its
geography (we noted the very precise delimitation of boundaries in the
ninth eclogue), but Marot wants purely literary effect. Colin pastures *deux
trouppeaulx*, not because this is the symbolic responsibility of shepherds
or because of any responsibility at all, but, rather, because it is in the reci-
pe, a convention the potential meaning of which Spenser never exploits.
  In Marot's imitation of Virgil's flower catalogue from *Eclogue II*, pas-
toral is a decorative and ornamental rhetoric; Marot has no special interest
in man's right relationship to nature. At a most characteristic pastoral mo-
ment, Marot unselfconsciously abandons country fiction for courtly
reality:

Portez au bras chascune plein Coffin
  D'herbes & fleurs du lieu de sa naissance,
  Pour les semer dessus son Marbre fin,
  Le mieulx pourveu dont ayons congnoissance!
                    (225-28)

The tomb of *marbre fin* has the same artful and unnatural status as the "sta-
tues polish'd by some ancient hand" that substitute for the genuinely pas-
toral, live fauns and fairies who inhabit Marvell's meadows in *"The Mower
Against Gardens."* Indeed, the flowers heaped *bien espays* upon the tomb
of Loyse are for show of courtly abundance, not for intrinsic meaning.
When Corydon selects flowers for Alexis, he performs with tenderness and
intimacy a dramatic representation of man's oneness with nature. Both his
erotic feelings and his vision of Alexis are contained in the phrases:

ipse ego cana legam tenera lanugine mala
castaneasque nuces, mea quas Amaryllis amabat.
addam cerea pruna; honos erit hic quoque pomo;
et vos, o lauri, carpam et te, proxima myrte,
sic positae quoniam suaves miscetis odores.
                    (51-55)

(I too will bring you quinces white with down,/Those chestnuts which my

Amaryllis loved,/And waxy plums: plums too deserve this honor;/And you,
O laurels, and your friend, the myrtle /Are to be mingled for your redolence.)

The first-person active verbs *legam, addam, carpam*; the *ego, mea, vos,*
and *te*; and the mingling of *suaves odores*, all testify to interrelation-
ships between man and nature. Virgil honors the *pomum* (a generic
name for "fruit" that here refers to *cerea pruna*), by the values within
the pastoral world; thus he makes the fruit itself proud and animate. To
the contrary, when Marot calls for *Lys blancs honnorez*, he speaks to
the values of the readers' world—grammatically, "*honnorez,*" a verb in
the past participle, suggests tacitly, "honored by us." Indeed, Marot
writes courtly language with a tone of relief; he describes the courtly
Elisium of Loyse with its *nayves maisons* (201), *nobles espritz* (308),
and immortal pet *Papegay* (212). So Marot both limits himself to a rhet-
oric and violates his own limitations—and the violation is naive, not
ironic.

Spenser, by contrast, opens his poem to include the reader's world,
while maintaining pastoral decorum. This he accomplishes by three
identifiable rhetorical techniques: he asks open questions of the reader;
he asserts meaning in aphorisms; and, perhaps most significantly, he
systematically heightens his rhetoric as his poem progresses toward sat-
isfactory universality. The first technique is evident in a comparison of
the frame of the November eclogue with Marot's eclogue. Marot treats
more amply than Spenser the tradition of gift exchange, but both main-
tain the preliminary debate that distances reader from dead figure:

Et si tes Vers son d'aussi bonne mise
Que les derniers que tu fis d'Ysabeau,
Tu n'auras pas la chose qu'ay promise,
Ains beaucoup plus & meilleur & plus beau;
De moy auras ung double Chalumeau
Faict de la main de Raffy Lyonnoys . . .
                    (Marot, 37–42)

An if thy rymes as rownd and rufull bene,
As those that did thy Rosalind complayne,
Much greater gifts for guerdon thou shalt gayne,
Then Kidde or Cosset, which I thee bynempt . . .
                    (Spenser, 45–48)

Marot moves predictably from his first promised gift, *des coings* (35), to
a gift of more value (*meilleur*) because the singing has exceeded expecta-
tion. The reader must then translate the worth of *ung double Chalumeau*
into the sophisticated literary judgment for which it stands. But Spenser
moves from the Kidde or Cosset to "much greater guerdon"—an open-

ended reward that rises logically from pastoral convention, although it is not particularly pastoral language. This openness raises directly significant questions about the values of poetry, poetic fame, and even patronage. (These were the issues of the preceding October eclogue with its talk of "prise," "prayse," and price.) The reader does not have to "translate" pastoral reward into literary judgment. Each reader may himself define "greater guerdon."

A second technique by which Spenser expands his pastoral rhetoric is to treat the theme of death in the pastoral world as though all deaths are alike. This he accomplishes by building aphorism from elegiac pastoral convention: nature's growth is cyclical, human patterns are linear; we grow toward death. These aphorisms, formulaic assertions about the true state of human affairs, are set down in a formal syntactic structure. They are separable from the body of the poem and belong to the reader as well as to the singing shepherds:

> The braunch once dead, the budde eke needes must quaile . . .
> (91)

> All musike sleepes, where death doth leade the daunce . . .
> (105)

> O trustlesse state of earthly things . . . nys on earth assuraunce to be sought.
> (153)

Here pastoral neither limits the range of sentiment nor requires a translation from simple to sophisticated values. Spenser is speaking his own language of pastoral.

The third technique, the gradual heightening of pastoral rhetoric, explains the originality and satisfaction of the poem. It begins in the early stanzas of the elegy itself with the characterization of Dido as a local, simple English flower gone from country society:

> The fayrest floure our gyrlond all emong,
> Is faded quite and into dust ygoe.
> Sing now ye shepeheards daughters, sing no more . . .
> (75-77)

Except for the placement (for emphasis) of the phrase "our gyrlond all emong," this is easy Spenserian verse. In the following stanza, however, Spenser asks a question that refers to death in nature, Dido's death, and to other deaths as well:

> Whence is it, that the flouret of the field doth fade,
> And lyeth buryed long in Winters bale:

Yet soone as spring his mantle doth displaye,
It floureth fresh, as it should never fayle?
But thing on earth that is of most availe,
    As vertues braunch and beauties budde,
    Reliven not for any good.
        O heavie herse,
The braunch once dead, the budd eke needs must quaile,
        O carefull verse.

                                              (83–92)

We read the first two lines of verse thinking that Dido is the "flouret of the field" now described in more formal language—"the" is substituted for "our"; "floure" becomes the more delicate, stylized "flouret." The peculiar "of" gives a slightly Bibical tone. This is still pastoral, but it is higher and more philosophical and questioning, with its strong interrogatives. In the fifth line, however, we discover that Dido is not the "flouret" at all but, rather, in contrast, is a member of the inclusive group—"thing on earth . . . of most availe." (The omitted article before "thing" elevates and opens the rhetoric further.) There is a difference between nature and human nature. But this is not as sad as one might suppose. Dido transcends the earlier level of straightforward pastoral rhetoric; she is "vertue's braunch," the moral offspring of metaphoric pastoral. Then, in a brilliant and ultimate elevation of the stanza's pastoral in the final aphorism, the human, linear pattern dominates nature; this human braunch and budde do not revive. (For a comparison with Sidney's use of metaphor in the line "Mountains of huge despair" from "You Gote-heard Gods," see chapter 3.)

These stanzas present an eclectic, "mingled" rhetoric, and a philosophical realism. The impact of death is neither softened nor accommodated in a world like the Virgilian rustic one, nor is it ignored, as in Marot's aristocratic milieu, where it becomes an excuse for extreme flattery and ornamentation. The final movement of the poem opens Spenser's language further by engaging the reader in the Spenserian act of combining "high" philosophy with rough, Anglo-Saxon vocabulary and rustic character. (The April eclogue uses this technique well, praising highest Queen Elisa in a rough Chaucerian voice.) In "November" the double rhetorical levels renew the reader's intimacy with one, singular, death, and simultaneously universalize death beyond limits of place or social class.

In the stanza below, located more than two-thirds of the way through the elegy, Spenser boldly combines tenderness and familiarity, the tone of mother questioning child, with ritualistic sonorities:

But maugre death, and dreaded sisters deadly spight,
And gates of hel, and fyrie furies forse:

> She hath the bonds broke of eternall night,
> Her soule unbodied of the burdenous corpse.
> Why then weepes Lobbin so without remorse?
> O Lobb! thy losse no longer lament,
> Dido nis dead, but into heaven hent.
>
> (161–67)

But the simple, "O Lobb" comes only after the grandeur of "She hath
the bonds broke of eternall night," after references to the dreaded fates,
the gates of hell, and the "fyrie furies forse," at the opening of the same
stanza. The revered mythic and archetypal machinery of death asks for
awesome, uncomprehending human response, then draws that response
toward understanding. With the line "Her soule unbodied of the burden-
ous corpse," the verse, too, lightens, justifying asking why Lobbin weeps
by presenting the question in diminutives and monosyllabic phrases.
With a friend's death the world may seem to die—Spenser's "mingled
rhetoric" gives play to the duality of this response.

The transitional reversal stanza "O trustlesse state of earthly things"
(154) has prepared us for this harmony of singular and universal by a
series of aphorisms, Chaucerian in tone and sentiment, which force us
from looking *outward*, across class boundaries, limits of private and
public, to looking *upward*:

> O trustlesse state of earthly things, and slipper hope
> Of mortal men, that swincke and sweate for nought,
> And shooting wide, doe misse the marked scope:
> Nowe have I learnd (a lesson derely bought)
>   That nys on earth assuraunce to be sought:
>   For what might be in earthlie mould,
>   That did her buried body hould,
>   O heavie herse,
> Yet saw I on the beare when it was brought
>   O carefull verse.
>
> (144–53)

The words "state of earthly things," "mortal men," "on earth," and
"earthlie mould," make all lives one, shepherd an equivalent for man,
and Elisium or heaven the only other place. Death has equalized us;
in the penultimate stanza of the elegy we are called "unwise," "wretch-
ed men," "fooles" for not recognizing that Dido represents our own
possible blessedness, our own power to transcend—"Dido is gone a-
fore (whose turne shall be next?)" (193). Elisium, the simple, pure
pastoral place of fresh fields and green grass is, for us, an available
metaphor—a *state* of mind—and also a reality, by Dido's habitation
in it.

This poem has gathered significance in its changes from one pastoral world to another, from one rhetorical level to another, from a troubled mourning to "Make hast . . . thether to revert" (191), from "heavie" to "happy hearse," from careful to joyful verse. The phrase "my woe now wasted is" (201) sums up the process; the recurrent word "wasted" has two meanings—first, in the process of the poem, all resources for mourning have been expended; second, the poem has been cathartic and engaging, so further woe is unuseful, unneeded. Woe for Dido's death is wasted (with its dual significance) woe for all. The pastoral rhetoric has been equal to the most profound of human events, moving us from a song chosen to accord man's mood and season's change to a deliberate mediation with forces larger than, though encompassing, nature's cycle of change.

iv

The term "pastoral rhetoric" refers to Spenser's play with varied pastoral ways of talking. "Rhetoric" attends to verbal intimacies of verse (particular word choices), to the shapes of phrases or to syntactic structures as they mirror ideas, and, finally, to the ideas and their shapes per se. The June eclogue talks about and in several pastoral rhetorics, using the problems these rhetorics raise and the poet's dissatisfaction with his performance of them to discuss the idea of ill-success in poetry and love. The poem identifies a simple, rustic pastoral; an elaborate, mythological pastoral; and the countryside, social pastoral that I have already linked with Rosalind.

The June eclogue addresses itself directly to the pastoral themes set forth in "January"—love, care, piping, and style. But from the narrow personal complaint of that poem, it moves to June foison, broadening these themes into what seems, at first, a chaos of confused chronologies, epic and Christian figures, ephemeral landscapes, and opposing poetic inspirations. If there is a narrative to be found, it is something like this: Colin and Hobbinol, like the two shepherds in Virgil's first eclogue, live in contrasting worlds—the first is an alien wanderer and the second is protected in his simple landscape. Colin explains his disconnectedness variously. In youth he could both love and sing of love, but age and time have made him reject performance as presumptuous and out of tune with historical circumstance. He indicates, however, that if he could sing, he would complain directly to discourteous and fickle Rosalind. Hobbinol expresses sympathy and indicates nostalgia for Colin's former "silver sound," but is not much practical help.

Hallett Smith summarizes the poem otherwise: "In the act of bewailing his sad state, he [Colin] says he is not able to continue, and instructs the other shepherd (inferior to him in ability at complaints) to tell Rosalind what she has done."[15] Smith's summary is instructive because he fails to trust the surface of Spenser's verse or to consider that if narrative does not emerge perhaps it is because Spenser did not intend it to. To make an appropriate musical analogy, expecting mono-dy, Smith refuses to hear polyphony. The shape and depths of "June" are as complex as a fugue in which successively entering voices deepen the music. The single, simple voice of the opening returns, enriched, at the end. In my reading of "November" I paid particular attention to the way in which Spenser opened his verse to his reader, and also began to define the elements of Spenser's "mingled rhetoric." This reading fur-ther isolates and orders the rhetorics, then explains how they function as polyphony.

To understand the function of rhetorical levels, it must be under-stood that the poem is not primarily a series of chronological narra-tive acts joining character and place, but, rather, a series of poetic moments. The mind of the dramatic speaker Colin, connected to no permanent biological landscape or geographical place, is autonomous, must confront its own powers, and must struggle at each moment with changing but self-created landscapes.

Similarly, Milton's "free" Satan and his Adam and Eve, rooted in the "place" of the garden, represent two possible relationships between man and landscape. For Adam and Eve, the unselfconscious acceptance of geographical limitation removes part of the burden of self-definition; garden tasks ask to be done, vines to be pruned, fruit to be plucked. Satan, on the other hand, holds responsibility for his own history, claims his mind is unattached to landscape:

> Hail horror, hail
> Infernal world, and thou profoundest Hell
> Receive thy new Possessor: One who brings
> A mind not to be chang'd by Place or Time.
> The mind is its own place, and in itself
> Can make a Heav'n of Hell, a Hell of Heav'n.
> (I, 250–55)

Recognizing no definition from place or time, Satan must face the fear-ful freedom of self-created, thus self-judging, values.

In the June eclogue Spenser hardly sees Colin as an "overreacher," blasphemous and magnificent in Satan's style, but he does grapple with poetry's power to create autonomous places in the mind. His reference, as I show below, is not to Virgil's *Eclogues*, but, rather, to the *Aeneid*, a poem in which the hero's journey and his song are, in an important way, an attempt to make coherent, and thus useful, his own fragmented history and his own lack of a home. Thus Spenser abandons the fiction of a real landscape and narrative to establish, in distinctive pastoral rhetorics, varied psychological moments and poetic worlds; these compete with each other and, by the poet's own aesthetic values, are judged insufficient to appease the longings of the mind, to make the mind an adequately fulfilling place "unto itself."

The poem begins in a simple, conventional *locus amoenus*, what the December eclogue calls Pan's "greene cabinet" or the "hurtlesse pleasaunce." The distinction of this landscape is that it is self-selected, a place to which the speaker has been enticed from other shades. The poet hints that it has emblematic status:

> Lo Colin, here the place, whose pleasaunt syte
> From other shades hath weand my wandring mynde.
> Tell me, what wants me here, to worke delyte?
> The simple ayre, the gentle warbling wynde,
> So calme, so coole, as no where else I fynde:
> The grassye ground with daynte Daysies dight . . .
>
> (1-6)

It is a site "as no where else I fynde" because the place has qualities much like those of the unfallen garden. The mind, weaned from wandering, harmonizes with an uncomplex nature. The attractions of the site are listed in simple, direct vocabulary and syntax. Air, winds, grass, and flowers characterize not the nature that set Colin in relief in "January," judged and anatomized by the "moral" vocabulary of his landscape, but, rather, the nature of one-dimensional, calm solitude. The rhetorical question "What wants me here?" *has* an answer: nothing else.

In responding to Hobbinol, Colin complicates the poem's music by making the green cabinet specifically a place of the mind. According to Colin, what Hobbinol has selected is not a site, but, significantly, a state:

> O happy Hobinoll! I blesse thy state,
> That Paradise hast found, whych Adam lost.
>
> (9-10)

The garden state is just the opposite of Colin's wordly discontent. And his restless journeying, his feeling of being pursued from coast to coast is just that—a feeling, a psychological state. The visual image has no narrative function.

Hobbinol next advises a change of place:

> Then if by me thou list advised be,
> Forsake the soyle, that so doth the bewitch.
>
> (17-18)

The reader may still believe that Colin will find peace if invited, in the mode of Christopher Marlowe's "Come live with me," into the garden world.[16] But in characterizing Colin's present world and presenting an alternative, Hobbinol abandons the idea of the simple, unfallen garden, and so changes tone and rhetoric that it becomes apparent that in this poem there are, so far, three pastoral worlds; each is a state of mind. The description of Colin's world reads like a child's Hallowe'en nightmare full of evil, primitive fears. Without shelter (Spenser uses the word "harbrough" [19] or harbor, presumably to carry through the image of being pursued from coast to coast), the restless mind lives among night ravens, elvish ghosts, and ghastly owls. On the other hand, the attractions Hobbinol proposes in the dale belong to the elegant, mythic, and pagan garden. This highly literary *locus amoenus* has no connection to the bewitched night landscape that precedes it. Hobbinol describes a daylight drama in which nymphs who "chace the lingring night" parade across the stage with rapidity to prepare for Pan, Phoebus, and more dancing and piping.

Colin counters Hobbinol's suggestion with still another version of pastoral, another rhetorical level—the Virgilian rural social world of Alexis and Corydon (*Eclogue II*)—identified in the January eclogue. Significantly, Colin's response, which is not in a mythological rhetoric, indicates his interpretation of that alternative mythological world, not as a place, but as a psychological and poetic moment. Such a moment is of the past; he connects it nostalgically with the pastoral of the plenteous English countryside where there were "Queene apples unrype" (43), gaudy garlands, and dalliance with a simple Rosalind from the neighbor town. The pattern of rhetorical levels denies us chronological narrative but substitutes in its stead a counterpoint of states or moods. In the December eclogue the rhetoric of the Virgilian social world stands, similarly, for a mood consistent with the pleasures of mythological pastoral. In that poem, too, Colin's nostalgic recollection of a youth free from the pain of love invites him to describe how he hunted the hare to tame it, gathered nuts, scaled the craggy oak, and sang so confidently that Pan yielded.

Yet Colin here claims that none of these distinctive rhetorics provides a pastoral appropriate to his mind. He calls them "former follies" (37) and "weary wanton toyes" (48); he dismisses "Parnasse hyll" (70) and chooses, instead, rough, "rudely drest" (77), self-pleasing pastoral. The rejections take place because of the poet's changing and ripening judgments of value for his own poetic skill and his own life course. "Time in passing weares" (38), he says, and, with a trace of irony adds that it "draweth new delightes with hoary heares" (40). The subsequent movements of the poem deepen our conviction that the poet hears rustic and mythological pastorals as impoverished voices because, as each rejected rhetorical level reappears, it is amplified and again judged an unsatisfactory place for the mind, a limiting voice of poetry.

Hobbinol begins the central section of the poem (l. 49) with two stanzas of conventional praise of pastoral poetry; the first stanza relates directly to Hobbinol's "pleasaunt syte," the simple *locus*, now filled out and more alive:

> Colin, to heare thy rymes and roundelayes,
> Which thou were wont on wastfull hylls to singe,
> I more delight, then larke in Sommer dayes:
> Whose Echo made the neyghbour groves to ring,
> And taught the byrds, which in the lower spring . . .
> (49-53)

The second stanza amplifies the world of mythological pastoral, using the *topos* of the poet's song astounding or silencing the Muses:

> I sawe Calliope wyth Muses moe,
> Soone as thy oaten pype began to sound,
> Theyr yvory Luyts and Tamburins forgoe:
> And from the fountaine, where they sat around,
> Renne after hastely thy silver sound.
> (57-61)

Colin dismissed the earlier songs as being unable to create a new place in the mind, a tranquil *state*; these praises he also dismisses, undercutting Hobbinol's decorative language (which is reminiscent of the *Epithalamion*) by his low tone, his simple, flat understatement: "Of Muses, Hobbinol, I conne no skill . . . " (65).

The five stanzas that begin with the denial of skill treat the function, goals, style, and inspiration of poetry in what appear to be contradictory assertions. But the great human poignancy of the honest phrase with which the passage ends—"But since I am not, as I wish I were"—should warn us that neat logical structures are not necessarily poetic truth. Colin's answer to Hobbinol's praises does not test the "narrative" consistency or the logic of conventions—responding nature, mute Muses, and inherited laurels—but, rather, explores conventions as poetic and psychological moments, asks whether they have been well-enough performed and understood.

There is little here of the narrative structure of the January eclogue. We should not and, appropriately, cannot logically reconcile Spenser's assertion that when he walked "withouten lincks of love" (34) he also piped plaintive pleas for Rosalind, who presumably he *did* love (41).

Nor should we force logic upon Spenser's claims for piping a low pastoral piano and against "flying fame" (75) as, supposedly, being consistent with his next indication. His voice should be a pastoral forte:

> I soone would learne these woods, to wayle my woe,
> And teache the trees, their trickling teares to shedde.
>   (94–95)

In contradiction to self-pleasing plaints, his songs should fly to his love, be published abroad, in order to condemn Rosalind and treacherous Menalcus:

> Then should my plaints, causd of discurtesee,
> As messengers of all my painfull plight,
> Flye to my love, where ever that she bee . . .
>   (97–99)

The poetry is about poetic skill, about making verse do what you want it to. These five verses of Colin's, beginning "Of Muses, Hobbinol," demonstrate plasticity in pastoral tone and theme.

The low tone (for example, "I conne no skill") is not simple, felicitous pastoral verse, as it is in the *locus amoenus*, but verse representing the moral choice to pipe modestly since neither more elaborate mythological and Virgilian rhetorics meet the poet's own standards. The element of moral choice is evident in the evaluative vocabulary—scorn, rebuke, presume, praise, blame, strive, win, pass. That such a moral choice figures in selection of a rhetorical level shows how deeply connected are the poetry and the world it represents, how much being what one wishes to be is like writing as one wishes to write.

The December eclogue also deals in great depth with the problems of creating one's own place in the mind through piping and singing. It creates, first, the fullest Virgilian rhetoric, complete with the poet's confident assertion about his own poetry ("To Pan his owne selfe pype I neede not yield" [46]), its unselfconscious limitation to a place ("My hurtlesse pleasaunce" [51]), and its easy choices between "pleasaunces," rather than between good and bad ("When choise I had to choose my wandring waye" [62]). Finally, the antitype to this satisfying fullness appears in a harvest of sterility:

> And thus of all my harvest hope I have
> Nought reaped but a weedye crop of care:
> Which, when I thought have thresht in swelling sheave,
> Cockel for corne, and chaffe for barley bare.
>   (121–24)

Moral choice is opposed to random or arbitrary selection from equal alternatives; self-consciousness is opposed to the mind defined by a place. Such moral judgment is mirrored in language. In Colin's speech in the June eclogue, self-consciousness is marked by direct syntax, harsh alliteration, such as "But feede his flocke in fields, where falls hem best" (75); by predominance of such colorless Anglo-Saxon words as "conne," "bene," "holden," "homely," "sith," "hem," "sittes," "wotte"; and by a deliberate rejection of high, mythological rhetoric. Pan and Phoebus *ornamented* the pastoral world at lines 30 and 31:

> And Pan himselfe to kisse their christall faces,
> Will pype and daunce, when Phoebe shineth bright.

But at line 70 their story is read as a moral indictment against singing competition. The familiar modesty *topos* quoted here even carries a submerged hint of Midas' asses' ears:

> For sith I heard, that Pan with Phoebus strove . . .
> I never lyst presume to Parnasse hyll.

The poem has other such judgmental repetitions. For example, the "low" and moral rendering of the "shade" *topos* gathers meaning from three other uses. Hobbinol uses "shade" as a metonym for "pleasaunce" or place: " . . . whose pleasaunt syte / From other shades" (2); in the other two instances it describes the pastoral place: "in Sommer shade" (44) and "in shady leaves" (54). But it becomes heavily moral, takes on overtones of secrecy, privacy, and humility when it is placed between emphatic "lows" and after Parnasse hill: "But pyping lowe in shade of lowly grove, / I play to please my selfe, all be it ill." (72). Shade is no longer a pleasant choice but, rather, a moral imperative.

The verses that concern the death of Tityrus represent Spenser's ideas of how a rhetoric should function and also amplify our notion of the poet as judge. In selecting Chaucer as "soveraigne head / of shepheards all" (83), Spenser selects the master of a vital but not particularly pastoral style. Chaucer, however, has significant, twofold successes. First, his poetry can, in Spenser's view, change the "place" of the mind:

> Well couth he wayle hys Woes, and lightly slake
> The flames, which love within his heart had bredd
> (85–86)

It can also entertain others, keep order in the world, and communicate to readers and listeners:

And tell us mery tales, to keepe us wake
The while our sheepe about us safely fedde.
                    (87–88)

Spenser thinks of these qualities only as wishes—"as I wish I were"—for himself and tells about them in the conditional. The place creating function is "I *soone would* learne these woods, to wayle my woe"; the communicating function is "Then *should* my plaints . . . flye to my love."

After acknowledging his defeat, Spenser, in Colin's voice, retreats to a simple, narrative rhetoric that discounts Hobbinol's differentiation between geographical places (hills and dales) and asserts again that his restless mind has no place. His verse tells about emotion rather than expresses it:

But since I am not, as I wish I were,
Ye gentle shepheards, which your flocks do feede,
Whether on hylls, or dales, or other where,
Beare witnesse all of thys so wicked deede:
And tell the lasse, whose flowre is woxe a weede . . .
That she the truest shepheards hart made bleede.
                    (105–11)

Hobbinol's answer is delicate and empathetic, though it confirms Colin's claims about himself and his inability to transform his situation. Hobbinol speaks in the unadorned, direct rhetoric of Adam, but does not suggest, as he did in the first lines of the eclogue, that Colin can move into Paradise:

O carefull Colin, I lament thy case,
Thy teares would make the hardest flint to flowe.
Ah faithlesse Rosalind, and voice of grace,
That art the roote of all this ruthfull woe.
But now is time, I gesse, homeward to goe:
Then ryse ye blessèd flocks, and home apace.
                    (113–18)

Indeed, he distinguishes himself from Colin by relieving man of some of the responsibility for shaping his own destiny, thus solving the problem of the mind and a permanent place. "A mediation occurs between the mind's desire for independence and the claims of divine authority . . . when we recognize that certain human characteristics or qualities may be left in the realm of the unaccountable."[17] The verse tells us that Rosalind is faithless, which means disloyal, as well as profane; she is void of grace, which means ungentle, as well as being not of the elect— hardly qualities that Colin can alter, or for which he is responsible. Nor are Hobbinol's flocks blessèd because he has made them so. Like the little drops of inspiration that the poet would have flow on him, blessèdness has a *deus ex machina* aspect that Spenser recognizes but that Colin cannot acknowledge.

Spenser has made demands on the possible rhetorics of pastoral that indicate not only his dissatisfaction with them but also his facility for reproducing them with just the "passing skil" that he insists died with Tityrus. This kind of tacit undercutting of the poet's humility is a familiar poetic technique. It appears, for instance, in *Astrophel and Stella*, where Sidney's indictment of "inventions fine" (I, 6), "strange similes" (III, 7), "Allegory's curious frame," "eloquence," and "philosophy" (XXVIII, 1,9,10), accompanies his having just produced them. The rejection of these techniques in favor of simplicity—"looke in thy heart and write"— is a conceit that allows the poet to have painted phrases and straight talk simultaneously. But Spenser, in a sense, takes this idea more seriously, goes beyond the tricky conceit that rejects elaborate convention for an equally conventional simplicity. His voice acknowledges aphorism and convention as the formulations of basic human truths. Spenser rejects the pastorals of pristine purity in Eden, the rural Virgilian social world, and elaborate mythology, not because they are meaningless, but because he cannot perform them with the skill necessary to create an adequate place for the June season's restlessly wandering mind.

v

In the April eclogue Spenser integrates and increments pastoral rhetorics and finds his own pleasing (and, perhaps, self-pleasing) style. The poem has none of the somewhat eclectic jarring and clashing of the June eclogue, although the various voices identified above persist. "April" manages to intertwine its voices in the service of praise for Queen Elizabeth and to the benefit of a distinctive English rooted in national identity, a language of which pastoral lyric and miscellany verse are the best examples. My analysis of "April" focuses specifically on language, in order to isolate the origins of this particularly effective voice and to determine the response it evokes in the reader. Necessarily, the question of Spenser's archaism arises, directing the discussion toward etymologies and the problem of Spenser's philosophy of language.

"Festive comdey," says C. L. Barber in *Shakespeare's Festive Comedy*, has intimate connections with one of the "principal forms of festivity, the May games . . . [in which] the bringing home of May acted out an experience of the relationship between vitality in people and nature."[18] As insular folk ritual developed into stylized native tradition, a literature with a dual nature emerged. The play or poem of "May" can be both a description of a May-day celebration, mirroring and thus preserving in the monument of literature the customs of a people, and a representation, in selective language, of vitality of spirit, the metaphoric complement of vital custom.

The language of tripping home with freshly plucked blossoms describes both an act and a spirit. If the act is rooted in native mores, so also is the language, as an exploration of some "Maying" etymologies demonstrates. Such linguistic vitality prevails in the August song of Bonibell with its characteristically charming phrases like "bouncing Bellibone" (61), "tripping over the dale" (63), "Kirtle of greene" (67), "sweeter then the Violet" (72), and "as clear as christall glasse" (80). The vital tone finds its way into poems of *England's Helicon* like "The Passionate Shepherd to his Love": "A cap of flowers, and a kirtle/Embroidered all with leaves of myrtle." The Elizabethan dramatists favor it in their songs. Shakespeare's version from *Love's Labour's Lost* shows the characteristic freshness: "When daisies pied and violets blue/and lady-smocks all silver white" (V, ii, 904-5). Seventeenth-century lyricists, too, chose native English vocabulary, despite their sophisticated, urbane use of pastoral convention. Robert Herrick sets an example, mingling man and nature in this artful line from "Corinna's going a-maying": "Rise and put on your foliage, and be seen/To come forth like the Spring-time, fresh and green,/And sweet as Flora." Similarly, in "The Coronet," when Marvell portrays the magnificent struggle between the serpent and the Saviour, the "I" voice employs festive language to evoke the vital, pagan pastoral world: "I gather flow'rs (my fruits are only flow'rs)/Dismantling all the fragrant Towers/That once adorned my Shepherdesses head."

In the April eclogue, Spenser perfects his English festive voice. In part, his success is based on the convincing naiveté of his narrator who simply invites us, in democratic fashion, to join him on the "grassie greene" (55). He points out "this blessèd brook" (37), tells us in the present tense, "I see Calliope speede her to the place,/Where my Goddesse shines" (101-2), and says excitedly, "Lo how finely the graces can it foote" (109). But even more significantly, this blazon of Elisa interweaves the fresh festive English I have just defined with both Christian and literary and mythological pastoral voices.

The cluster of words that establish the religious element and make Elisa Christian, angelically beautiful, and virginal never emerge as explicitly as those which call her English May queen or pagan goddess—presumably because of pastoral decorum and because a Protestant would not emphasize the blessèdness of the Virgin. (Spenser's concession, perhaps, is the singular "God" in line 51.) Nonetheless, the cluster is unmistakable. The words are listed here with their frequency of occurence in the poem. Several words have etymologies in Old English or Middle English and thus call up specifically English names for theological concepts.[19] They are: blessèd (2)—OE blēstian; Virgin (3); heavenly (4)—OE hēofen; grace (4); angelick—from ecclesiastical Latin; without spotte—ME lyrics, *The Pearl*. While these words may be used in mythologized description—as if we were to say awkwardly "angelic Pan" or "blessèd Venus"—they must move us toward the Christian or theological layer of meaning by the associations tied to their primary definitions.

The vocabulary of literary mythological words appears in names—Nymphs, Parnasse, Helicon, Pan, Syrinx, Phoebe, Cynthia, Latona, Niobe, Calliope, Muses, Chloris. In this vocabulary Christian overtones are absent; Elisa is the classical shining (101), beaming (76, 84) goddess. These clusters are mingled and interwoven with the primary, fresh English vocabulary of Elisa, the rustic shepherdess. For example:

> Pan may be proud, that ever he begot
>   such a Bellibone,
> And Syrinx rejoyse, that ever was her lot
>   to beare such an one.
> Soone as my younglings cryen for the dam,
> To her will I offer a milkwhite lamb:
>   Shee is my goddesse plaine,
>   And I her shepherds swayne,
> Albee forswonck and forswatt I am.
>   (91–99)

Greek Pan, surrogate for Christian God, begets (a word with Biblical overtones) an English country maid. E. K. glosses "Bellibone" in its own vocabulary: "Homely spoken for a . . . Bonilasse." So simple and countrified is this derivative from French *bonne* and *belle* that Spenser plays with its morphemes in the August eclogue: "I saw the bouncing Bellibone,/Hey ho Bonibell" (61). The flat juxtaposition of Greek "goddesse" to English "plaine" repeats the pattern; it is countrified further with Anglo-Saxon "forswonck and forswatt" both Chaucerian in tone. But plain rhetoric can also include other, nonmythological, nonreligious words such as "tawdrie laces" (135), "primrose" (62—late ME), and "gelliflowres" (137—ME gilofre). These words make Elisa, first, queen of the English spring and, second, virgin and pagan goddess. These words have the rustic charm that pervades English verse but defies precise definition.

I suggested earlier that homely English flower names might have a special power in linking vitality in man and in nature. The catalogue of flowers in the April eclogue is a particularly rich example of English rustic charm. My method, suggested by Martha Craig's fine article "The

Secret Wit of Spenser's Language,"[20] will be to determine from the etymologies of flower names and from their associations for the reader, the particular world they define. Craig argues persuasively that Spenser adhered to a rationale for vocabulary choice, derived from Plato's *Cratylus*, in which "words must be not merely conventional and arbitrary . . . but 'correct' and 'true,' . . . [in which] the etymology or true word is not historically true, but philosophically true."[21] Such a theory speaks more fruitfully about the fully developed language of *The Faerie Queene* than it does about *The Shepheardes Calender*, but, in modified form, it is useful to us. The statement that "words reveal reality through their etymologies . . . words contain within them little self-explanatory statements"[22] puts in precise language a pregnant insight into the Renaissance reader's approach to language. Further, words are emblems of specific ideas; a word was perceived as a sound, not as a printed "picture"; a word's identity was not "inextricable from its spelling." Thus, "'sun' and 'son' are for us two different words which sound alike," while for Donne, for example, they are one word, one utterance with two meanings denoting, together, "the Second Person of God and the fire of heaven."[23] The Renaissance reader, then, was accustomed to words having several meanings and associations.

Flower names take on their homely tone by calling up in the reader rustic rather than botanical or "learnèd" associations. This can happen in two ways: 1) Flower names derive from rural English itself, having origins in spontaneous country fancy like May festivity; they display imagination in fixing analogies in nature; or 2) Flower names have changed from technical Latin botanical tags into common forms by aural transposition. Phonetic modulation destroys the "learnèd" root and makes a direct correspondence between name and flower; no cluster of associations intervenes. Here intermingled are examples of both types:

> See, where she sits upon the grassie greene . . .
> Upon her head a Cremosin coronet,
> With Damaske roses and Daffadillies set:
>> Bayleaves betweene,
>> And Primroses greene,
> Embellish the sweete Violet . . .
>   (55-63)

> Bring hether the Pincke and purple Cullambine,
>> With Gelliflowres;
> Bring Coronations, and Sops in wine,
>> Worne of Paramoures.
> Strowe me the ground with Daffadowndillies,
> And Cowslips, and Kingcups, and loved Lillies:
>> The pretie Pawnce,

> And the Chevisaunce,
> Shall match with the fayre flowre Delice.
> (136–44)

An example of the first type is "cowslip" from "OE cuslyppe from cow-slyppe, viscous or slimy substance, i.e. cow slobber, cow droppings." Others might be bachelor's-buttons, crow-flower, dead man's fingers, honeysuckle, lady's-smock, larks' heel. Read as self-explanatory statements, each has two meanings and multiple associations. Each is a distinct flower species and, simultaneously, the thing named. In order for us to be in sympathy with the reader who heard these flower names, we should think about a mind that did not hear 'son' and 'sun' as a pun. Certainly, today we do not dissociate completely the flower from the qualities given in its name—bachelor's-buttons or lady's-smock may look like the objects for which they are named. The subtle but crucial difference is that today we do not consider the doubleness to expose an intrinsic, mysterious, or organic connection between meanings. Shakespeare barely brings doubleness to the surface: "Nay, I am the very pink of courtesy./Pink for flower" (*Romeo and Juliet*, II, 3, 62). Unavoidably, cow droppings arrive with the gift of cowslip to Queen Elisa, and morbidity with dead man's fingers. To use such names in poetry is to be in touch with a kind of primal, earthy energy in nature, more refined but analogous to "Bulluc sterteth, bucke verteth/Murie sing cuccu!"[24] But to use such names is also to touch and reaffirm a kind of piquancy that allows the human world to name flowers and, by naming or objectifying them, to render the associations of the names benign.

Daffodil, daffadowndillies, or daffadillies, an example of the second possibility, can only be flowers: "Daffodil from asphodel. Alteration with unexplained 'd' of med. L. *asfodillus*, var. (simulating a diminutive formation) of late L. *asphodelus*." The learned associations—*asphodel*, genus *Narcissus*—have disappeared (as they have not from the common French *asphodèle, narcisse des prés*), leaving only the simplest of relationships between the yellow flower and its common English name. So also for "pawnce" or pansy from the French *pensée*. An Ophelia who has read one of the popular books that associated flower names with human qualities brings the association to the surface: "And there is pansies—that's for thoughts" (*Hamlet*, IV, v, 177). "Gelliflowres" is OF girofle, or ME gilofre, altered to the final "flower" by usage, though still *giroflé* in modern French; "flowre delice" is the French fleur-de-lis, but the *lis*—lilly—Latin *lillum* equivalence has been lost, and a fanciful Latin root in *flos deliciae* substituted. E. K. delightfully confirms the confusion: "Flowre delice, that which they use to misterme, Flowre de luce, being in Latine called *flos delitiarum*."[25]

When the flower name no longer defines botanical grouping (as "delice" does not designate lilly, *lis*, or the genus *Lilium* but, rather, stands for a certain flower), then the poet or singer can alter or play upon the structure of the word as long as identity of name with flower is clear. Such wordplay might explain the variants daffodilly, daffadowndilly; pensy, paunsie, pawnce; gillyflower, gelliflowre, July-flower; flower de lice, flower delice, and a Spenserian and Shakespearean modification, flower-de-luce. A similar line of reasoning could explain the playful English quality of Bellibone and Bonibelle.

The untaught, country truths of the flower catalogue affirm the mingling of rhetorics in a kind of linguistic democracy. In the absence of learnèd associations the reader has assented to touching humility and has permitted uniquely English nature the authority to deck a queen. Barber further suggests a kind of reciprocity between queen and English nature: "The whole conception of gathering in the powers reigning in the countryside to yield them to Elizabeth, and of Elizabeth vivifying the countryside by her magic presence . . ."[26] means that Elizabeth gives dignity to humility and simplicity in the best pastoral way.

English freedom to play confidently with nature and nature's descriptive words has no parallel in French pastoral. There, poetic language and peasant language are intentionally separated—the former, high, elegant, written vocabulary; the latter, vulgar speech without charm. Du-Bellay's highly literary "D'un Vanneur de blé aux vents" produces a feeling of rusticity by using diminutives as terms of "endearment," but the poet remains in the world of formal poetic speech. He plays with the *botanical* or sophisticated names:

> J'offre ces violettes,
> Ces lis et ces fleurettes,
> Ces vermeillettes roses,
> Tout fraichement écloses
> Et ces oeillets aussi.
>
> (7–11)

Other French poets use diminutives, too, as Marot does in "De la rose" with its singular vermilion rose; the Pleiade's plea for simplicity, however, produced few catalogues of picturesque or homely flower names to adorn pastoral. What tonal differences appear between the *roses, lis, belle marguerite*, and *oeillet* of Ronsard's "Elegi à Henri II" and the flower catalogue in "Lycidas" with its homely primrose, crow-toe, musk rose, cowslip, and daffadillies?

Besides English flower names, other peculiarly English words, some of which make up the basic level of rhetoric in the April poem, support the notions of nationalism in language and linguistic democracy. Such words are: "worthy," "semely," "blotte," "lively chere," "modest eye," "deffly," "soote," "meriment," "begot," "plaine," "forswonck," "forswatt," and "deck." Along with "forswonck" and "forswatt" (Chaucerian borrowings), these words bespeak their Anglo-Saxon origin, their disparity from elegant French or latinate vocabulary. This vocabulary, managed here with consummate skill, holds down the rhetorical level of pastoral, keeps rusticity while using mythological and Christian vocabulary to give high seriousness and dimension to conventions of the mode. This artfulness permits Spenser simultaneously to deify and not deify Elisa; Elisa represents equally valuable simple modesty and majestic divinity, each setting off the other. Empson is correct—Spenser's is a harmonious doubleness, he says, commenting specifically on *The Shepheardes Calender*, "in which Elizabeth is appropriately the daughter of Pan . . . Spenser makes the thing safely playful by mixing it both with myth and pastoral."[27]

This doubleness permits the narrator to speak in country voice; it also extends the linguistic democracy into the philosophical structure of the poem. Two particularly skillful minglings of rhetoric show the possible unity between conceptual structure and linguistic level. At line 133 the narrator addresses the shepherds' daughters:

> See, that your rudenesse doe not you disgrace:
> > Binde your fillets faste,
> > And gird in your waste,
> For more finesse, with a tawdrie lace.
> > (133-36)

With an exquisitely ironic touch, Spenser uses the elegant French *finesse* that asks the shepherdesses to dress like French ladies, but that finesse, or the absence of rudeness, does not produce French elegance; rather, it sanctions and elevates the rustic English style in "gird," "waste," "tawdrie," and "lace." Thus fineness gets its definition from the narrator, who approves homely apparel and indicates that it has the specialness due a celebration for Elizabeth. The narrator has unified majesty and simplicity.

The second example of playful doubleness derives specifically from Elizabeth's inseparable person and rôle:

> 'Tell me, have ye seene her angelick face,
> > Like Phoebe fayre?
> Her heavenly haveour, her princely grace,
> > can you well compare?
> The Redde rose medled with the White yfere,
> In either cheeke depeincten lively chere.
> > Her modest eye,
> > Her Majestie,

Where have you seene the like, but there?
(64-72)

In each juxtaposition of descriptive words, rhetoric and rôle intertwine.
Christian "angelick," heavenly, and grace touch and shade Elisa's royal,
princely, face and "haveour." In a brilliant example of vocalic (rather
than orthographic) determination of meaning, "modest eye" includes
the meaning "modesty" and, certainly, also the "ie"-"eye" morpheme
of "majestie." With the phrase "lively chere," "modest eye" and "majes-
tie" present the rustic, country version of royal, divine pastoral. In a
sense, Empson's analysis of the way in which pastoral "upper" and
"lower" plots comment on each other in Elizabethan drama can explain
the poetic coexistence in the stanza above. But rather than developing
into irony and full-blown dramatic ambiguity—the line of Empson's dis-
cussion—the two "plots" form a unity.[28]

Michael Drayton imitates, in part, Spenser's April eclogue, but he
fails to mingle rhetorical levels effectively. His strained "Third Eclogue"
in *Idea, The Shepheardes Garland*, beginning "Rowland, for shame,"
exists in versions of 1593 and 1619 (revised as *The Third Eclogue* of
Pastorals). In the 1593 poem, overt religious allusion—"that foule, seven-
headed beast" (l. 120)—destroys the delicacy of unstated Christian
allegory, but the "high" rhetoric that replaces the phrase in the 1619
version is equally ungainly. Drayton shifts gears into heroic with an
awkward reference to "Albion conqueroring the Appenines" (l. 120).
He succeeds better in capturing the native English tone in these lines,
which remain in both versions:

And crave the tunefull Nightingale to helpe them with her Lay
The woosell and Throstle-cocke, chiefe musike of our May.
(64-65)

His flower catalogue, however, betrays uneasiness with the Spenserian
homely phrase "daynte Daffadillies" (1593), which he replaces in 1619
with a confusion of both etymology and flower: "see that there be store
of lillies,/Called of Shepheards Daffadillyes." Even less successfully, he
changes the phrase "sweetest virelayes" (1593)—which is, at least, a neu-
tral one—to the jarring French-English phrase "dapper virelayes"; but
his song is neither formal virelay (a fixed French song form)—indeed, he
also calls it roundelay (another fixed French form)—nor is it dapper
(smart, trim in homely English rhetoric), as an analysis of its 14-syllable
rhythmic pattern illustrates.

If Drayton admires Spenser's democratic linguistic eclecticism, E. K.
misses its significance. In his "April" notes he talks embarrassedly about

rudeness being indecorous and issues apologies for homely rhetoric:
"Binde your [fillets]) Spoken rudely." "Homely spoken"; "When Dam-
sins) A base reward of a clownish giver." He reads rustic, Christian, and
mythological voices separately, unable to integrate with them the vital
voice of nature purified by Elisa's presence. Indeed, he trembles before
Elisa, and thus seems to misinterpret the final lines of the song:

> Now rise up Elisa, decked as thou art,
>   in royall aray:
> And now ye daintie Damsells may depart
>   echeone her way,
> I feare, I have troubled your troupes to longe:
> Let dame Eliza thanke you for her song.
>   (145-50)

The narrating voice addresses first Elisa, then the damsels, and, finally,
asks the queen to reciprocate—to thank the troop for singing to her. But
E. K. transposes the roles of the actors—"For having so decked her with
prayses and comparisons, he returneth all thanck of hys laboure to the
excellencie of her Maiestie."

I set out to define the particularly effective native English tone of
the April eclogue, and can conclude that the charm, in part, derives
from a quaint vocabulary, a forthright use of the language of freshly
blooming primroses and grassy shades, and the secure intermingling of
Christian and mythological references. Syntactic and stanzaic structures
that enforce such integration are discussed in the final section of chap-
ter 3.

In this chapter, my comments have been primarily about style, about
vocabulary choice and the particular responses that specific choices call
up in the reader; there are larger questions to be answered. The intimacy
with nature that permits Spenser to invite the queen into his landscape,
the intimacy of that same queen in declaring that she reciprocates in the
love of her people, implies control over nature and human nature re-
spectively, a control for which linguistic security stands merely as a
small reflection. The illusion of voluntary intimacy is achieved at the
cost of the mind putting a specific construction on the world it chooses
to inhabit. In Spenser's secure rhetoric lies a selectivity that permits
man to control his landscape. The following chapter explores the rela-
tionship between man and nature in *The Shepheardes Calender* and
attempts to determine the construction Spenser put on the world a-
round him.

CHAPTER 3

Spenser's Pastoral Landscape:
The Mind's "Myrrhour"

In a calendar, the natural passing of time is accounted for and organized according to a system found by humans. Indeed, the calendar imposes a form of control on nature because humans assign meaning to nature's patterns of growth and change. For the farmer, the calendar is a mediator between the inexorable progress of time and his own ability to cultivate the land in timely fashion. The calendar, as Spenser might say, attempers the farmer's endeavor to the season. For Spenser, however, the calendar had little touch with seeding, fertilizing, cultivating, or harvesting. He seized the calendar form because the human organization of nature's patterns—the calendar's meaning—can be used to accommodate man to his *own* life experiences, as in this characteristic passage from the December eclogue:

> So now my yeare drawes to his latter terme,
> My spring is spent, my sommer burnt up quite:
> My harveste hasts to stirre up winter sterne,
> And bids him clayme with rigorous rage hys right.
>   (127–30)

Even the sometimes obtuse commentator E. K. understands this use of nature as a source of explanation for human behavior; he says, in the Argument to "December," "Colin . . . proportioneth his life to the foure seasons of the yeare." Spenser turns nature's patterns of seasonal change into emblematic mirrors that confirm the timeliness, not of seeding and harvesting, but of common human emotions and experiences.

The title *Shepheardes Calender* apparently derives from the *Calendrier de Bergers*, a kind of sixteenth-century *Poor Richard's Almanac*, which sets out for each month the tasks a farmer must do if he is to live from the land. Planting, sheep shearing, and pruning schedules are the order—each connected to its appropriate zodiac signs and interpretations. Spenser's *Calender* stands as well in an elaborate and sophisticated tradition of sculpture and manuscript illumination. Indeed, the most numerous analogues for Spenser's methodical connection between month and human activity, calendar time and psychological time, are found in the visual arts. Besides the almanac source of the calendar idea, Spenser had pictorial reality.

In the late medieval period, through the thirteenth century, favorite subjects of sculpted small-scale design were the signs of the zodiac, each accompanied by a human figure performing a task appropriate to the season depicted. On the façade of Amiens Cathedral, for example, there stands, for June, a human figure binding sheaves of wheat; for August, a man who seems to be plucking either grapes or olives. In each portrait extended landscape is nonexistent or depicted only to specify the labor—in June, baled and unbaled sheaves, in August, a single tree.[1] May, the month of leisure, is illustrated by "a man resting under a flowering tree, and the Zodiac sign of the Twins . . . turned into a pair of lovers."[2] These figures engaged in everyday occupations are depicted with a spareness that causes the twentieth-century viewer some difficulty in interpretation but suggests how common the month-agricultural-activity association must have been to the medieval person who stood at the church door.

In the early fifteenth century man set himself in a more fully realized landscape, as for example, in the lushly illustrated calendar pages of the *Très Riches Heures du Duc de Berry*. February, a snow landscape, shows "sheep huddled together in their fold, birds hungrily scratching in the barnyard, and a maid blowing on her frostbitten hands."[3] In a brilliant, sunny October scene with a splendorous château in the background, a grim, downtrodden peasant in torn clothing scatters seed. The January scene of the *Très Riches Heures* depicts the castle interior where the duke is feasting. The warmth of the colors and the bustle of activity about the banquet table suggest that the artist has enough confidence with convention to assume that his viewer would know that winter chill may be symbolized or evoked by its opposite—the protective interior.

In the best of Spenser's pastorals the calendar idea is pushed beyond the visual artist's symbolism to its end point; the representative mind creates fictional, seasonal landscape outside of itself that reflects and accommodates inner psychological states. In poetry this distinction appears as a poise between literal description of nature and nature used as pure metaphor. This complex use of nature in the service of human nature is the key to Spenser's pastoral and the subject of this chapter. I explore here in detail the March eclogue, which opens with an appropriate seasonal landscape; that landscape becomes a vehicle for exploring the life stage of early spring. I analyze, as well, the August sestina, which opens with nature already turned to emblem, and the November and April eclogues, in which landscape is humanized in keeping with seasonal convention—and beyond convention.

The March eclogue illustrates Spenser's exploration of the true dimension of the convention of the awakening of erotic desire in springtime. In the perfunctory and conventional summary of the poem, E. K. tells us: "Two shepheards boyes taking occasion of the season, beginne to make purpose of love and other plesaunce, which to springtime is most agreeable." But the central mode of the poem is to equate March with adolescence, with marvelous lightness and humor, to create a "landscape" of the teenage mind. The poem, mirroring the mind, builds meaning from small detail, anecdote, and deft movements of verse rhythm. The young singer Willye questions the sorrow of his friend Thomalin and discovers that its source is Thomalin's knowledge that ' lustie love . . . is abroad at his game" (26). Willye offers to watch Thomalin's sheep in return for a favor—that he describe his encounter with love. In the story, Thomalin, on holiday with other shepherd "groomes," shoots into a rustling bush and precipitates a pitched battle with Cupid, who inflicts upon the tender young man a rankling love wound. With charmingly abstract innocence, Willye affirms, from what his father said about love, that yes, indeed, love wounds are a source of woe. Then "stouping Phebus" urges the lads homeward.

ii

In a critique of the *Variorum Spenser*, Leo Spitzer analyzes the March eclogue, which he thinks to have been "wrongly appraised."[4] His interpretation depends on his reading of Bion's *Idyll IV* and Ronsard's *Ode* of 1556 (later called *L'Amour oiseau*), poems Spenser followed. I agree with Spitzer that modifications of and additions to these sources show that the poem's meaning is to provide an experience of the awakening of adolescent love. "With Bion," Spitzer tells us, "the fowler boy seeks to capture what seems to him to be a huge bird though the poet has informed the reader that the creature is Cupid. When the youth, his forces spent, finally gives up the chase, he goes to seek advice from the old ploughman who has taught him the art of fowling—to learn only that he should shy away from that particular bird." Bion maintains a double perspective in which the reader and the old man know the bird as the demigod Eros, but the child does not. Indeed, the delicate joke of the poem—its intent—is to set the child apart. Only the reader knows "an epigram such as: 'do not prematurely seek to fall in love.'" The poem "paraphrases an intellectual epigram quietly addressed, over the head of the child, to the adult mind."[5]

Ronsard focuses his attention on the bird, which takes on a dazzling outward appearance, but against whose "sinister essence" the boy is warned by a pessimistic old fortuneteller. Spitzer asks of Ronsard's poem, "do we not have the familiar baroque pattern of 'sensuous beauty unmasked': a pattern in which illusion and disillusionment . . . are presented with equal insistence?" While for Ronsard's boy, Eros is identified by name, the poet merely uses him to play off innocence against experience. "He is told by his informer that the *meaning* of love ('*que c'est que d'aimer*') will become clear to him only in the future, through personal experience which he can not have at his age."[6] Again, the poem merely expands our adult experience.

Spenser's poem not only explains adolescent nascent eroticism but provides an experience of it as well. No learnèd elder intervenes with an elusive explanation and the element of duality is eliminated. "With Spenser it is the lad himself who learns the identity of the winged being—as the result of being pierced, in his pursuit, by Cupid's shaft."[7] He recounts his experience to another adolescent, so the tables are turned. We listen to the children talk, not to the adults explain. Spitzer sums up the poem in one sentence, which moves us from innocence through the experience of enlightenment: "In this inimitable *poetic description of puberty*, we are led, in an uninterrupted sequence, from careless sporting in nature to the chase of an elusive something, which turns out to be Love, then to the struggle with the god which ends in defeat, and to a lasting wound."[8]

The change from winter sorrow to pleasant spring establishes the delicate energy of beginnings:

> Seest not thilke same Hawthorne studde,
> How bragly it beginnes to budde,
>   And utter his tender head?
> Flora now calleth forth eche flower,
> And bids make ready Maias bowre,
>   That newe is upryst from bedde.
> Tho shall we sporten in delight,
> And learne with Lettice to wexe light . . .
>   (13-20)

Here, as elsewhere, nature speaks the language of human nature and demonstrates the poet's appreciation of male sexuality. The Hawthorne "studde bragly (boastfully) buddes," it has a "tender head"; the flowers are "newe upryst." Learning to love Lettice is also part of the spring landscape—she is Donne's "lovely, glorious nothing," the revelation of "Aire and Angells," any feminine name among infinite possible names to be fit to a still anonymous love object. Learning to love Lettice is learning to identify and feel pleased by one's

own eroticism; it is also an experience of first love pain, of yearn-
ing.

After the spring frame, the process of learning to identify Cupid re-
peats itself in the body of the poem in a competitive and adolescent
debate:

> Thomalin: Willye, I wene thou bene assott:
> For lustie Love still sleepeth not,
> But is abroad at his game.
>
> Willye: How kenst thou, that he is awoke?
> Or hast thy selfe his slomber broke?
> Or made previe to the same?
> (25-30)

Is little love awake or asleep? He's awake. Then prove it. Willye shows
the excited impatience of all first talk about sex: "Now tell us, what
thou hast seene" (60). For though it is to be Thomalin's story, Willye,
too, has heard about the birds and bees—appropriately, from his father:
"For once I heard my father say" (105). But this father, like most, had
only discussed theory; his Cupid was unarmed:

> Tho sayd, he was a winged lad,
> But bowe and shafts as then none had:
> Els had he sore be daunted.
> (112-14)

Thomalin's story of his encounter with laughing, leaping Cupid fur-
ther unfolds his innocent mode of experiencing the world. The process
of identification shows his ingenuousness, his lack of expectation. Some-
thing of the tone of nursery rhyme or fairy tale prevails in such phrases
as "For birds in bushes tooting" (66) and "I heard a busie bustling" (69).
The verse is full of small movements, mock-heroic, as Hallett Smith puts
it,[9] but sympathetic rather than satirical. We share Thomalin's hurt sur-
prise when, in the space of four lines, he feels a "little smart," which "in-
creases," "rankles more and more," and, finally, "inwardly festers"; the
child's phrase of one syllable words—"ne wote I, how to cease it" (103)
—comes from a first discovery of nonphysical hurt in a formerly benign
world.

Adolescent psychology and budding eroticism are Spenser's interests
in this eclogue, but the growing child does not stand in any specially
valuable relation to nature. Spenser's boys are not like the children of
Blakes's *Songs of Innocence and Experience*, nor are they like Lewis
Carroll's Alice, whom Empson portrays as innocent swain, nor—closer

historically and thematically—are they like Marvell's "Little T. C. in the Prospect of Flowers" who, innocent as a young girl, will one day be a harsh Petrarchan mistress.[10]

The great moments of *The Faerie Queene*—Redcrosse fighting despair and the dragon, Amoret in the house of Busyrane, Venus and Adonis, the rescue of Serena—prove that Spenser respects maturity; age brings human heroism and fulfilling love, neither of which is gained without the kind of pain that teaches. It is the awakening into pain and pleasure that Spenser associates with normal adolescence. The brilliance of his explication comes because nature is neither a setting for awakening nor an ornament. Poised between literal description and pure metaphor, landscape mirrors adolescent qualities of mind, for example, as Spitzer shows, the quality of dormancy.

> The statue of the god Cupid clad with ivy is then the symbol of that mythical weddedness of nature and art that is presented as an age-old or timeless element in the pastoral convention. But the presence of Cupid in nature in the form of a statue has a dormant quality—the god is potentially, not actually present as if sleeping 'in Lethe lake.' And it is perhaps in order to emphasize the state of oblivion in which the god dwells before he has become actual and 'awake' that Spenser has introduced the ivy instead of the Greek box-tree (which Ronsard has preserved . . .). Surely Spenser's change is to be explained by a desire not only to acclimate our episode to England, but also to enforce the 'dormant' aspect of Love: the evergreen ivy which is independent of the seasons is usually associated by us with the past, with ruin, with the grave: it represents nature spinning its age-old web of oblivion over the slowly decaying works of man; the statue of Cupid covered with ivy represents then the minimum of Love's effectual force. But out of this state of sleep, Thomalin will 'awake' the god.[11]

Removed from the usual stylized sonnet setting, the poet makes the love wound convention yield its unexpected perspective on youthful naiveté.

iii

In the following analysis of the sestina from the August eclogue, several stanzas from "April" and "November," and the February eclogue, two points become more precise. First, if nature is static, a reflective mirror rather than a process of movement, then nature can mirror paradox and irresolution truthfully. Second, if nature is a creation of the human mind, it can be willing witness to a variety of human states; man can put *his* construction on nature.

In the August eclogue, says E. K., "is set forth a delectable controversie" that consists of two songs. In the first, two singers alternate lines and their performance is judged by a third "umpire." The second song is one of Colin's doleful plaints performed by a solo singer, Cuddie. The festive spirit and light lyric form of the first song oppose and contrast with the serious evaluative concerns of the second song—melancholy, suffering, and self-analysis. The contrast of light and festive with dark and heavy makes form a symbol of mood; the poems themselves represent conflicting possibilities that join paradoxical human emotion to a transitional season of the calendar year. Where the first song comes to resolve overtly unmediated grief by the overwhelming form and tone of holiday celebration and the presentation of prizes to both singers, the second song, the sestina, suggests by its content that grief remains unresolved—form and tone reinforce sadness.

Hobbinol's simple *locus amoenus* in the June eclogue represents man and nature harmonious; the mind, weaned from wandering, "inhabits" a tranquil place. In that poem Colin, not Hobbinol, anatomizes nature as a poetic resource for human emotion. Similarly, the August eclogue assents to a secure, unified, unquestioned relationship between man and nature in the first song, but complicates the status of man in nature in the sestina, a distinctive "Colin" landscape, labeled immediately as such by Colin's own melancholy vocabulary in "wastefull," "witnesse," "plaints," and "carelesse." Our focus, then, is Colin's complex relationship to himself and, thus, to nature, one controversy within the larger delectable controversies of the contrasting songs.

In Colin's absence Cuddie sings his song; characteristically, little narrative emerges. The singer, rejecting "resort of people" and the domesticity of "the house" since his love has departed, claims the "wastefull woodes" as witness of his woe. He vows to remain complaining in that landscape until Rosalind returns. That the chronology of the love affair and its fate interest Spenser little and Colin's experience of pain interests him most is attested by the absence of fact. Why has Rosalind left? Will she return? We don't know. And no factual clarity comes from Colin's comparison of himself to the female nightingale who complains for memory of "hys misdeede." Colin's broken spirit has priority over his (or Rosalind's) crime.

The sestina, a highly restrictive form, serves Spenser's purpose of deepening the meanings of words and emotions; its main vehicle is repetition. With its requisite economy of language, one would expect schematization and precision. Sir Philip Sidney's double sestina "You Goteheard Gods" fulfills these expectations and presents a schematic change in landscape and human emotion. David Kalstone defines one aspect of structure by analyzing the movements of Sidney's poem. In "a magnificent crescendo" the poem "moves from an opening memory of past joys through a violent climax of despair." An analogous movement takes place in the use of landscape: "The elements of landscape take their places metaphorically as part of the inner world of fancy and lose their status as solid objects."[12] The real "grassie mountaines" of line

one turn into metaphoric "mountaines" of "huge dispaire" in line six-
teen. The poet turns the real pastoral world of potential richness to a
metaphoric representation of barrenness. Finally, when he compares
man and nature, he makes pastoral simile into a decorative, expressive
language and pastoral arrives at its artificial and allegorical status. Thus,
for example, the "shee" for whom the two singers mourn "did passe in
state the stately mountaines,/. . . to whom compar'd, the Alpes are
vallies" (63, 67). Stately mountains are real in the fiction of the poem's
world but when they are compared to "shee" their stateliness becomes
a representation of the lady's statuesque qualities, her majesty. Moun-
tains are no longer primarily real. When "Alps" become "Vallies," how-
ever, Sidney has precisely and schematically turned a metaphor into
another metaphor and elevated the symbolic level twice, so that nature
is neither real nor psychological, but literary and decorative. The des-
criptive, individualizing aspect of stateliness disappears—alps equalling
valleys can only be a metaphor for extravagant praise, a decoration of
the lady with the unimaginable. Such extravagant, purely allegorical
praise is the mode of the common festive lyric.

   Spenser's poem exhibits no such change and moves continually on
the middle level. Nature never has the status of object, nor does it rest
on the fiction of simple decoration. We experience the sestina as a sus-
tained, only slightly modulated moaning; the poet's plaint and a respon-
sive, integrated nature are constants. Spenser's first words, "Ye waste-
full woodes," assume, as Sidney's did not, that the natural world is
already a metaphor for inner feelings. As in the January eclogue, "waste-
full" speaks evaluatively, puts a human construction on nature. On the
surface, "waste" has a judgmental meaning—woods perform no useful
function and are void of value. Far beneath stands the descriptive, neu-
tral meaning derived from *vastus*: "empty land." Nor does "wasteful"
describe Colin; rather, his word choice mirrors his mind, "pictures"
his self-image, and is an example of the rhetorical use of pictorial
diction. Similarly, the meaning of "carelesse byrds" (154) suggests
the continuum between man and nature, the sharing and building of
meaning to present a state of mind. When, some twenty lines later, the
line occurs, "Helpe me ye banefull byrds, whose shrieking sound/Is
signe of dreery death . . ." the similarity of "baneful" to "careless" in
both grammatical position and word character ("careless" is closer, for
example, to "baneful" than to other possible modifiers such as "sing-
ing" or "tuneful") allows one to shade and increment the other.

   Spenser never becomes a baneful bird as Sidney grows "a shrich
owle to myself" (18), because such a metaphoric level would destroy the
intermingling between man and nature and force the poem to become
allegory. That is, it is patently absurd to think of the literal meaning of

Sidney's language. He could have in mind only a symbolic metamorphosis that denies even the fiction of a flesh and blood "shrich" owl and simply makes nature "part of the inner world of fancy," as Kalstone suggests. Spenser, on the other hand, always retains the fiction of a natural landscape outside of the mind but reflecting and produced by the inner world. The edge on which Spenser's landscape poises itself is defined thus—the shrieks of baneful birds describe, pictorially so as to move the reader, a landscape, not an interior fancy; but the inner world is characterized by its selectivity, by the shrieks it chooses to hear and describe.

Spenser's poem is neither neat nor schematic; thus a certain exciting tension present in Sidney never develops, and a "violent climax" never occurs. In Sidney's poem oppositions of harmony to chaos, past pleasure to present despair, pastoral ease to nightmarish uneasiness, depend on a precise temporality and an exaggerated, artificial opposition between places that forces the poet to set limits and then to strain against them. The repeated terminations bear the burden. Empson describes the sources of tension. Monotony is, of course, comparative: the poem "beats . . . with a wailing, and immovable monotony forever upon the same doors in vain. Mountaines, vallies, forrests, musique, evening, morning . . . these words circumscribe their world."[13]

Spenser's terminations refer to human behavior, not to confining and changing times and places. "Woe," "sound," "cryes," "(a) part," "sleep," "augment" all mediate between singer, landscape, and audience. The first end word, "woe," sets an example; it builds a cluster of associations by its likeness to other words in the poem, which also deepen and define the singer's melancholy. Such words are "plaints," "cryes," "griefs," "doole," "pleas." Because woods (landscape) "witnesse" the woe and are "meet" for it, certain words describing woods clearly function also to further define woe. "Wastefull," "wide," "wild," and "gastfull" are reflexive, echoing, sounding and resounding, making the chosen environment an aural mirror of poetic emotion. Finally, the reader, who has been experiencing woe through the course of the poem, has defined for him through that word the distance at which he stands from Colin's suffering. In the first four stanzas Colin speaks of "my woe, my greater woe, my restlesse woe"; in the fifth stanza he uses "woe" not only as the appropriate termination, but also within the poem to disclaim that his cries have betrayed the "least part" of his woe.

Having performed the "inexpressibility topos," Spenser moves to set woe in the less personal context of myth—"hence with the Nightingale will I take part" (183) who remembers "hys misdeede, that bred her woe" (186). The final stanza affirms that even the exemplary woe of the nightingale, even a memory of woe, designates deeper suffering than that endured in the process of the poem by the reader. Directly, the reader is told *he* feels simply pity: "And you that feele no woe . . . pitie augment" (187,189). Such a plea speaks as much about the inadequacy of human communication, the isolation of suffering, as it does about the failure of poetic language to produce more than an imprecise approximation of human emotion.

The conflicts built in the poem concern not Sidney's transformation of benign nature to tortured human nature, an adept exercise in rhetorical change, but, rather, Colin's experience as melancholy singer of the song as opposed to that of the reader drawn into the performance. Thus the story, read from the end word "woe," has its larger analogy. The narrative thread tells us that the poet has left the constriction of the "walled towne" for the uncivilized expansiveness of the woods, more appropriate to his solitary and unlimited grief. There, in that melancholy place of the mind, he will remain until Rosalind returns life to normalcy. Then normal small-town diction—"safe and sound/She home returne" (180-81)—will replace pastoral melancholia. The audience and Rosalind inhabit the social world of bed and bower. They constitute the gregarious "you" who must be asked to "breake your sounder sleepe and pitie augment" (189). But the terminating words, compressed in the final tercet, intermingle the clusters of associations, the worlds of Colin and reader. Though Colin claims the reader feels no woe, the poetic structure denies it.

The final lines of the poem bring us full circle and broaden our perspective. Note the modification of rhythms below. Perigot, the festive singer, praises "doole" in heavy verse; Cuddie, the "dooleful" singer, turns nightfall into a time for lighthearted piping:

> Perigot: And Cuddie, fresh Cuddie the liefest boye,
>   How dolefully his doole thou didst rehearse.
>
> Cuddie: Then blowe your pypes shepheards, til you be at home:
>   The night nigheth fast, yts time to be gone.
>   (192-95)

The contrasts mirror, of course, the pleasurable and painful songs of the eclogue itself, this time intermingling them with finality. The two songs appear to be separate, but Spenser also indicates his desire that they be read as commentary upon each other, that the two landscapes of country dale and dreary wood and the two singers of holiday and everyday represent one truth, just as the month of August points both to fruition and death.

The August sestina maintains a landscape outside of the mind, poised between nature's reality and pure metaphor, that is clearly rhetorical in effect. The November and April eclogues, discussed below, push to their limits a nature representing inner fancy, yet they do not become purely metaphoric. Indeed, if Spenser ever admits his own pleasure and responsiveness to the natural world, if floods and flowers ever touch his heart, then it happens in these pure expressions of celebration and grief in "April" and "November." Significantly, these two eclogues humanize nature. Nature does not appear, in the Virgilian mode, as an echoing, lively, independent landscape, but, rather, as a tamed friend to man. In "November" nature is personified as Dame Nature; "April" simply withdraws her potentially threatening power.

In the Virgilian world of *Eclogue V*, when Daphnis dies, four-footed beasts neither eat nor drink; lions moan and wild forests speak. Presumably, the thought beneath the convention is that earth feels the wound; earth, as actor, makes unnatural events occur. Stress falls on *unnatural* because, for Virgil, nature has a constant, predictable being, an independent and implicit set of laws that, apart from man, determine the ways of the husbandman. Thus the range of unnatural events can encompass, along with obvious aberrations in animal behavior, seemingly "possible" changes in specific flora. In *Eclogue V* such a change demonstrates the power of nature to transform her own terms, to act independently of human vision:

> grandia saepe quibus mandavimus hordea sulcis,
> infelix lolium et steriles nascuntur avenae;
> pro molli viola, pro purpureo narcisso
> carduus et spinis surgit paliurus acutis.
> (36–39)

> (The furrows where we planted barleycorns / Yield worthless cockle and unlucky tares; / Instead of violets and gay narcissus, / Thistles have sprung up, and prickly briars.)

Virgil emphasizes the separation between human intention and the acts of nature in *mandavimus* and *nascuntur*; *we* sow, but apart from our vision of how nature *should* respond, barren oats are born. Similarly, the verb *surgit* in line 39 suggests that nature sets the terms of her biological processes beneath the earth, in the soil, beyond the purview of man.

For Spenser nature exists only insofar as it is a poetic servant of man, a way of speaking about human problems. In "November," the memory of nosegays is replaced by the reality of a world in the act of mourning, a world bent on transforming the orthodox presences of literary pastoral into human, speaking pictures of grief. The three stanzas beginning "Ay me that dreerie death should strike so mortall stroke" (123) and ending with the poet's pleas that his Muse mourn represent a modification of Virgilian convention and a specific construction of the pathetic fallacy. These stanzas, responding to Virgil's *Eclogue V* and Marot's *Elegie*, are based on neither notions of unnaturalness nor a distinct nature but are based, rather, on a human perception of a world transformed and created in the image of death. In "November," the undoing of Dame Nature's kindly course (l. 124) merely sums up what the observer's eye has already seen: the mind of the aggrieved mirrored in faded flowers (l. 109) and tones of black and gray (l. 107). Here, clearly, human death has power over a personified, sympathetic mother earth:

> Ay me that dreerie death should strike so mortall stroke,
> That can undoe Dame natures kindly course:
> The faded lockes fall from the loftie oke,
> The flouds do gaspe, for dryed is theyr sourse,
> And flouds of teares flowe in theyr stead perforse.
>   The mantled medowes mourne,
>   Theyr sondry colours tourne.
>   O heavie herse,
> The heavens doe melt in teares without remorse.
>   O carefull verse.
>
>   (123-32)

Trees have human locks, not leaves; Spenser maintains his familiar poise between floods of water and floods of tears, using the lines to express how much (floods are dry) mourning there is, how grief means, paradoxically, the draining of resources of expression and their simultaneous fullness.

The second mourning stanza of "November" moves from sympathetic landscape to animal sympathy. The rhetoric becomes more austere, more purely literary. The omission of two normal articles, in "feeble flocks in field" and "The beastes in forest," emphasize, not place, but inclusive poetic formula. These are all possible flocks, beasts, fields, and forests, from all pastoral landscapes. The world as a whole acts out grief, refusing usual activity, wailing and weeping—except for the wolf that, in chasing the wandering sheep, recalls to us the significance of having to wander, having no *place* except a melancholy place of the mind. Unlike Virgil, whose mourning nature is localized, whose plants are distinctly named species, and who demands from his reader a sense of wonder at the independent transformation of nature, Spenser creates a world that permits his reader to see through the eyes of the bereaved that death may be a benign human event when one believes that nature is "on your side," when one judges nature benevolent and sympathetic. Such a judgment is contained in sheep seeming to weep, beasts wailing, turtledoves lamenting, and the nightingale steeping her song with tears.

The third mourning stanza of "November" speaks directly to the April eclogue, undoing its festivities before our eyes, portraying nature at her most sympathetic, her most civilized, performing a ritual of lamentation. The fragmentation and disorder that successfully produced the liveliness of drama in process of being performed in "April" is gone from "November." Past experience is ordered; even grammatical structures form a pattern:

> I see Calliope speede her to the place,
>> where my Goddesse shines:
> And after her the other Muses trace,
>> with their Violines.
> Bene they not Bay braunches which they doe beare,
> All for Elisa in her hand to weare?
>> So sweetely they play,
>> And sing all the way,
> That it a heaven is to heare.
>> ("April," 100-108)

> The water Nymphs, that wont with her to sing and daunce,
> And for her girlond Olive braunches beare,
> Now balefull boughes of Cypres doen advaunce:
> The Muses, that were wont greene bayes to weare,
> Now bringen bitter Eldre braunches seare.
>> The fatall sisters eke repent
>> Her vitall threde so soone was spent.
>> O heavie herse,
> Mourne now my Muse, now morne with heavie cheare.
>> O carefull verse.
>> ("November," 143-52)

In "April" our eyes are directed to a circus of movements and activities—Calliope, the goddess, Muses, violins; then questions, music, critiques. But in "November," all is structured as inevitably as progress from season to season: "Nymphs . . . wont . . . to sing," "Muses wont . . . to weare," "Now balefull boughes . . ." "Now bitter Eldre"; and, finally, gathering the patterns together, "The . . . sisters . . . mourne now . . . now mourne." The figures are the same mythological pastoral ones, but the reading experience is not of festive celebration or a joyous moment but of orderly change. This kind of orderliness prepares the mind for acceptance of Dido's triumphant and final change in breaking the bonds of night to "Walke in Elisian fieldes so free" (178). Spenser's use of Virgil makes the point in little—for Virgil's seeds are planted, and grow unnaturally and bizarrely sterile, but Spenser's olives and bays do not disappear to grow up cypress and bitter elder. Nature obligingly provides the foliage appropriate to the moment and mood of the human mind.

The April eclogue, too, supports the humanizing of nature, here, refreshingly, to express joy. The frame of the poem moves us through the familiar relationship with nature—that in which nature shapes human feeling (April showers and tears)—to that in which nature is a neutral *locus amoenus* (Thenot and Hobbinol are "close shrouded in this place alone"). Once the song begins, however, nature becomes an active expression of man's confidence and security. The pastoral landscape has no peripheries, no localities, but not because the mind wanders (as it does in "June"), but because festivity rules; there is no monotonous "every day," nor is there an "other place" where dangers could lurk. Nature and man are continuous in a landscape of flourishing fields of gillyflowers, sops-in-wine for the shepherds' daughters, and nearby springs for the ladies of the lake.

The poem charts the withdrawal of threat from nature, from poet, and from the queen. In the April poem Thenot questions Hobbinol's sadness:

> Or bene thine eyes attempred to the yeare,
> Quenching the gasping furrowes thirst with rayne?
> Like April shoure, so stremes the trickling teares
> Adowne thy cheeke, to quenche thy thristye payne.
>   (5–8)

But sadness is made an essential and positive aspect of the cycle of nature in that "gasping furrowes" need rain; "quenching" is a restorative. (In "November," in the comparable but negative use of the cycle, human tears quench the gasping floods, but without restorative power, because "dryed is theyr sourse" [126].) April sorrow *does* restore both poet-singer and listener, the first by allowing him fulfillment in festive verse, the second by exposing our distance from sorrow in identifying with Hobbinol. His is a magnanimous sympathy at two removes. Hobbinol grieves for Colin as lover of scornful Rosalind. Colin's "madding mind" of which Hobbinol speaks does not taint the neutral shade or the well-behaved sheep who do not wander but "graze about in sight" (31).

In the blazon itself, idealized English countryside holds no threat. Homely, thus familiar and attractive, it is represented by the linguistic democracy of Spenser's festive language. Elisa sanctifies the landscape displaying her magical powers to transform (only ever so slightly, subtly) her environment into a symbol of the well-being she protects and maintains as queen. The blessèd brook, watery bowers, and grassy green make nature an ornament or jewel to adorn the pastoral garment. In this one happy instance, the mind has created a satisfying place, not an unselfconscious hurtlesse "pleasaunce," but a consciously joyful and significant garden.

In the April eclogue, Spenser's ideal appears in the superlative beauty of the three-personed queen; in her, tensions are resolved. Regent, Virgin, and Lady of May, Elisa, possessed of magical powers beyond those of Colin or Cuddie, stands for harmony. Nature needs no evaluative, moral vocabulary of her own because, in the spirit of the festive moment, and while presided over by a superhuman, unifying figure, mind and landscape are one.

iv

While the February eclogue further confirms Spenser's bias toward a definition of nature in human nature, it presents the special case of *The Calender*, the case in which literal description of nature *has* an allegorical translation, the special case in which a coherent dramatic narrative moves the reader forward in time. This fable, unlike those in the "religious" eclogues, depends on botanical resources to supply the pastoral figures. Thus it is remarkable that even here, in the tale of the old oak and the youthful briar, Spenser indicates that he would not have us read in dramatic terms, nor would he build anticipation by formulating questions such as: Which of the two trees will survive the winter? What is the moral to be read from the survivor? Rather, expressiveness supplants drama; we ask how Spenser will round out two states of mind. Further, it is remarkable that the subject matter of the eclogue that describes nature most thoroughly concerns her the least. Analysis of this eclogue will show that drama is secondary and nature "unreal" and that, despite plot and characters, paradox in human emotion has Spenser's interest.

The plot is simple. Old Thenot and young Cuddie dispute the virtues of youth and age until the former offers to tell "a tale of truth . . . cond of Tityrus" (92): two "characters," the deeply rooted, large bodied oak and the bragging briar embellished with blossoms, stand side-by-side. The upstart taunts the oak with his uselessness and argues that he should be gone because he provides neither fruit nor shade and even smells bad. The oak takes the criticism to heart. Arrives the husbandman, to whom the briar complains, presenting himself as the husbandman's martyred servant:

> So beate his old boughes my tender side,
> That oft the bloud springeth from wounds wyde:
> Untimely my flowres forced to fall,
> That bene the honor of your Coronall . . .
> (175-78)

He succeeds in silencing the forbearing oak and sending the husbandman home for his axe. The axe itself rebels against harming "holy eld," but the oak falls, shaking the earth. The briar survives, "puffed up with pryde" and unrepentant, until winter kills him off because he lacks the oak's protection. Cattle tred him underfoot. Cuddie claims no ease from the tale, and orders old Thenot to hye himself homeward.

The February eclogue explores in detail one common *topos*—the contrast between youth and age. The trees are nature's emblems, but this lengthy narrative portrays the relationship between man and nature by ignoring it. The pattern or structure of nature appropriate here, the change from youth to old age, is simply a given. The human intricacies of each state are not. These states attract Spenser.

The perfunctory seasonal opening sets up as primary contrasting consciousness and sensitivity; character is secondary, a vehicle. Thenot represents a state of mind called "Eld" and Cuddie, one called "Youth." Thenot never becomes a round dramatic character or even human enough to admit a process of change. Far from ever having had a young man's fancy, he suffers and serves timelessly:

> But gently tooke, that ungently came,
> And ever my flocke was my chiefe care.
> (23–24)

Cuddie, too, is static and never hypothesizes a future when his budding branch will be cropped. Spenser writes neither theoretically about the sequence of the ages of man nor abstractly, in the form of a Ciceronian *de senectute*. Rather, he asks how two ages differ as human experiences, how variously the world shall be served by them. He pits innocence against experience, pastoral dalliance against harsher husbandry, compelling beauty against useful virility, and even eclogue against georgic.

Cuddie's first speech constructs a winter landscape rooted in a physical nature. The wind and weather bite and blow and feelingly persuade Cuddie toward self-definition. The cold blows through his body as though his skin were pierced; his bullocks stand shivering in the wind. His similes exaggerate his feeling—the animals shake like "high towers in an earthquake" (6) when once they were "perke as a peacock" (8). Despite this physicality, specific winter landscape disappears. Spenser uses winter again, not for itself, but to focus on the issue of human sensitivity.

Thenot's answer to Cuddie immediately by-passes the issue of weather and moralizes against sensitivity or being indulgent of ungentleness. Thenot's phrase "to suffer the stormy time" (15) refers, not to weather, but to cosmic and inevitable life pain. Cuddie, too, immediately forgets February weather, and amplifies his own focus on sensitivity by turning winter storm into indisputable, time-honored metaphor:

"My shippe unwont in stormes to be tost" (32). He flaunts his "flow-
ring youth" (31), calling up erotic, vital strengths clearly absent from
old men.

Thenot's first speech hypothesizes that a reluctant harmony with
nature is the correct attitude for man. It sets man on a perpetually mov-
ing wheel of fortune that leaves him resigned, passive, and even deliber-
ately insensitive—somewhat like Wordsworth's Old Man (in "Resolution
and Independence") who lives reluctantly "not all alive nor dead/Nor
all asleep . . ." (64-65). Spenser emphasizes the determinism of the
cycle by a kind of repetitive incantation that makes change predictable
and even static:

> Must not the world wend in his commun course,
> From good to badd, and from badde to worse,
> From worse unto that is worst of all,
> And then return to his former fall?
> Who will not suffer the stormy time
> Where will he live tyll the lusty prime?
> Selfe have I worne out thrise threttie yeares,
> Some in much joy, many in many teares;
> Yet never complained of cold nor heate,
> Of Sommers flame, nor of Winters threat:
> Ne ever was to Fortune foeman,
> But gently tooke, that ungently came:
> And ever my flocke was my chiefe care,
> Winter or Sommer they mought well fare.
> (11-25)

Storm, prime, heat, cold, joy, tears, summer flame and winter threat,
gentleness and ungentleness all seem alike, set off by this sage in an
unchanging, melancholy past. In his own cosmic view he is an unindi-
vidualized part of a collective human nature, his mind, a summary of the
aphorisms of his civilization, his time on earth, like that of Wordsworth's
Leech Gatherer's, an unextraordinary point in the larger continuum.

Cuddie's response confirms a pattern of personal, present-moment,
individualizing talk—the alternative to this cosmic wisdom. Youth seeks
self-definition, individuality. Cuddie rejects harmony with nature, the
obliteration of self in the collective consciousness, and aphorism as a
mode of comprehension:

> But my flowring youth is foe to frost,
> My shippe unwont in stormes to be tost.
> (31-32)

The feel of Cuddie's verse is always reaction to the moment—his

mode of thought depends on specific examples, on the immediacy of
his language and syntax. Even his analogy between age and winter is
abrupt and unphilosophical: "This chill, that cold, this crooked, that
wrye" (28). He attacks, not old age, but this very man, old Thenot, des-
cribed before our eyes with "emperished braine" (54), "tottie head"
(55), and "corbe shoulder" (56). Nor does Cuddie allow love to be im-
posed upon by time's threat, though time orders Thenot's world, pre-
paring him for the inevitable future years. Thenot says, when you seem
free of fear, comes the "breme winter" (42); Cuddie lives for the mo-
ment and without a sense of doom—Phyllis is won for many "dayes"
(64).

Having used the seasons to establish two attitudes toward life, Spen-
ser moves on to make emblems of the attitudes themselves. Cuddie's
"ragged rontes," (5) initially shivering suddenly gain strength to ignore
the cold, for they represent Cuddie's view of himself; he has the fertility
and erotic strength of a young bull. His vivid similes—"his hornes as
broade as Rainebowe bent,/His dewelap as lythe, as lasse of Kent" (74)
—characterize the psychology of a young man in love with his own
sense of virility, bursting with energy. This is native English April rheto-
ric. Thenot's flock are deflated, sterile, deprived of sexual energy in their
widowhood. Their rhetoric is also of the English countryside, but it is
melancholy:

> Thy ewes, that wont to have blowen bags,
> Like wailefull widdowes hangen their crags:
> The rather Lambes bene starved with cold,
> All for their Maister is lustlesse and old.
>   (81-84)

Thenot counters this personal slur on his virility with a predictable and
impersonal aphorism: "Youngth is a bubble blown up with breath" (87).

In the one hundred lines of poetry that precede the pastoral fable,
alternate but not exclusive attitudes toward life are built through skill-
ful poetic techniques. While Cuddie argues against Thenot's stoic accep-
tance of vicissitude, suffering, and servitude, he is unable to obliterate
its essential rightness as a possible assessment of man's place in the cos-
mos. Though one might say that all the attractive lines have been given
to the spirit of youth, age-old wisdom holds its own equally with pas-
toral dalliance. Spenser does not build a pure and absolutely attractive
pastoral charm. The conventional pastoral world for which Cuddie
speaks appears through the antagonist's eyes: as if he were viewing
through a telephoto lens, Thenot describes something far off, precious,
a child's diminished landscape where little "herdgroomes" who crow
in corn pipes (40) are dismissed, paternally, as "fond flyes" (39). Cuddie

himself poses the advantages of his own world as an impossible and past condition: "But were thy yeares greene . . ." (59). This festive pastoral world is a temporary one. There is no single way in which man is served by the world, nature, or even landscape.

The technique of the fable itself defies the traditional view of narrative. The fable does not address itself to pastoral problems; thus, its setting is elusive. There are shepherds, garlands, nightingales, and blossoms to fix the festive pastoral world, and the domesticity of nuts, roast pork, a husbandman, and a solid old oak to fix the realistic rustic world, but the point of the husbandman has nothing to do with the right use of nature's resources by man; it has no ecological intent. The wielder of the axe acts in a drama on two levels; the literal problem, however is less important than (and is a symbol of) the parallel philosophical problem. On the philosophical level the singularly human and simultaneously abstract qualities of ambition (youth) and humility (age) are actors. The structure of this "dark conceite" or allegory makes nature stand for an idea separate from it. In other eclogues, the poise between literal and metaphoric levels provides a continuum in each direction, integrating landscape and idea. In essential ways, pastoral death is like all death, pastoral love pain like all wounds of the heart, but we cannot say, without the mediation of an explanatory device, that young men are like briars, old men like oaks. The narrative produces no dramatic interaction between man and man, no particular insight into human relationships. It simply uses character and nature as vehicles to present ideas.

Spenser's ideas are complex. He does not choose a large oak and a small one, but two different trees, just as Virgil chooses the analogy of the *cupressi* as opposed to the *viburna* to set Rome off from other towns.[14] Both trees are types of human nature, but how distinctly Spenser builds their presences! The briar, like the eclogue form itself, pleases by its vitality, its irreverence, it generic prettiness. It speaks in English country voice:

> Seest, how fresh my flowers bene spredde,
> Dyed in Lilly white, and Cremsin redde,
> With Leaves engrained in lusty greene,
> Colours meete to clothe a mayden Queene . . .
>   (129–32)

The oak, more like the georgic, presents harder, useful, yet awe-inspiring realities. Aeneas, in conflict between private life (Dido) and public life (the founding of his own city) is compared with the deep-rooted oak:

> ipsa haeret scopulis, et, quantum vertice ad auras
> aetherias, tantum radice in Tartara tendit.
>   (IV, 444–45)

(But the tree stands firm on its crag, for high as its head is carried/Into the sky, so deep do its roots go down towards Hades):

There grewe an aged Tree on the greene . . .
                                (102)

The bodie bigge, and mightely pight,
Thoroughly rooted, and of wonderous hight.
                                (106-7)

Here is dignity gained from deep experience; here is competition for festive rhetoric.

Hallett Smith, in summing up this eclogue, remarks that "the briar [finds] out when winter comes that it has been dependent upon the old oak. So the threat of winter and rough weather or old age, when time drives the flocks from field to fold, is the basic challenge to the pastoral ideal and must be faced."[15] But Smith reads the wrong analogies—and here they are tempting—seeing the fable as though it were "a fiction with a continuous double significance" or had a "clear allegorical translation,"[16] with the result that he must find age and youth present in every movement of oak and briar, and must produce, not the double emblems that conclude the poem, but a single moral. Age and time passing destroy *otium*. Spenser, as we have seen, is not interested in the processes of change in time or in season, nor is he talking about flocks, or what "must be faced." Rather, in the exploration of two states of mind, he produces, poetically, two experiences, one, light-spirited, brash, even narcissistic; the other, honorable, dignified, tempered, and sacred. In the end, the grandeur of the oak protects him no more than the lively self-interest of the briar. The mottos, taking opposite views of the godliness of old men, leave the conflict unresolved, true to human experience.

v

In the first sections of this chapter I suggested that Spenser portrays the human mind by making nature the mind's mirror. This use of nature is unusual enough to jar the reader into a fresh perspective on convention. As I have pointed out in passing, however, Spenser also attends to the effect of the rhythm, form, and tone of the voices within the poem on the listener without. This technical skill buttresses Spenser's meaning, and serves to control and structure the reader's responses by appealing less to his intellect than to his musical ear.

In John Thompson's *The Founding of English Metre*, Spenser is acknowledged as a metrical innovator in *The Shepheardes Calender*, but he is also taken to task because "the structure of the lines themselves is not always clear: sometimes it is impossible to say what Spenser's metrical pattern was, or even if he had one."[17] C. S. Lewis, like Thompson, singles out the April eclogue for particular criticism. "April is the strangest," says Lewis. "We begin with thirty-six decasyllabics and then have a Ronsardian ode. Long and short lines are mixed in a regular pattern and the first two stanzas have a regular iambic movement. In the later stanzas the short lines become irregular. . . . Some even of the longer lines cease to be plain decasyllables."[18]

Such criticism springs from several assumptions: first, that Spenser established a line length, stress pattern, and stanzaic structure that he later inadvertently ignored and second, that rigorous formality in making poetry makes inherently better poetry. But the April "laye of fayre Elisa," the musical poem—the song, the sweet sound, the "dittie" that Thenot requests, represents the best of *The Shepheardes Calender*. Its success depends not on the precision and formality with which Spenser follows a poetic prescription, as that for the French virelay, but on its musical conception. Spenser's is not a speaking voice, but a singing voice that has the liberty to embellish and ornament where it will. Like the Renaissance melodic line that attends to the caprice and fantasy of the vocalist, the April eclogue plays with its structural limitations and charms the listener by unpredictable variation. The rhythmic variations show that Spenser considered them an appropriate technique for maintaining the joyful, spirited movement and mood of his song. In the third stanza Spenser describes Elisa:

'See, whére she síts upón the grássie gréene
   (O séemely síght!)
Yclád in Scárlot, like a máyden Quéene,
   And Érmines white.
Upón her héad a Crémosin córonét,
With Dámaske róses and Dáffadíllies sét:
   Báyleaves betwéene,
   And Prímroses gréene,
Embéllish thé sweete Víolét.

                (55–63)

Except for a slight clash between meter and phrasing in "See"—the first word of the stanza—the first four lines are regular iambics. In line 59 we have an anapestic fourth foot in "cremosin," unless one reads the word with two syllables, which its variants suggest as a possibility. Line 60 clearly breaks the normative iambic pentameter. The effect is to separate roses and daffadillies into two clusters by forcing the reader-listener to change meters at the anapestic foot. So with "bayleaves" in line 61, which Thompson admits "probably breaks the order of stresses in the first foot."[19] Line 62 adds an extra syllable in its anapestic second foot.

And, in the last line quoted here, as Thompson says, the final word "violet" does not distort the stress pattern, but does distort "the pattern of the phrase . . . by the purely metrical stress on the last syllable."[20] Spenser could have easily kept his meter and syllable count by having singular roses in lines 60 and 62, or by omitting the "and" in line 62. Indeed, 16 of the lines in this 115-line song begin with "and," an often expendable word, used here to impose a change of rhythm, as in:

Strowe me the ground with Daffadowndillies,
And Cowslips, and Kingcups, and loved Lillies:
    The pretie Pawnce,
    And the Chevisaunce . . .

(140–43)

The omission of "and" (141) would reduce the syllable count from eleven to a standard ten. But its inclusion sets up the expectation or illusion of an unexhaustible supply of flowers.

If we move from rhythm to verse form, from the pattern within lines to structure itself, we note again a marriage between meaning and poetic process. "November," for example, builds a top-heavy stanza structure that helps to create the feeling of fulfilled expectation in the repetitive incantation of "O heavie herse,/O carefull verse." Unlike the April eclogue, it is absolutely regular in line length and meter, since its goal, in relation to the reader, is to capture him, to make him a servant to inevitability. The radical change to "O happy herse,/O joyfull verse" happens almost unnoticeably, fulfilling the expectation of the repeated short line, but also assuring the reader's assent to Dido's apotheosis.

The song of the Bonilasse within the August eclogue is an even more interesting case. Spenser sets up the expectation of a poem in amoebean form, or what Virgil calls, in his third eclogue, alternating verse. Traditionally in amoebean form, the second singer answers the first in an equal number of verses on the same theme; he tries to "cap" what the first has said by showing his superior singing skill. The contest is judged by a third party. While the three shepherds in the August eclogue pick Cuddie as judge, and any reader glancing at the page of print would see the alternating lines going properly back and forth between Perigot and Willye, in every way Spenser structures the poem to represent harmony rather than contention between singers.

The song sounds like a folk song. Instead of capping each verse of Perigot's in competitive fashion, Willye repeats and reforms Perigot's words. Every other line of Willye's is a simple five feet starting "hey ho." The narrative is strung together by Perigot, and Willye's additions, as in the verse quoted, only elaborate on what has already been said.

Or as Dame Cynthias silver raye
   hey ho the Moonelight,
Upon the glyttering wave doth playe:
   such play is a pitteous plight.
The glaunce into my heart did glide,
   hey ho the glyder,
Therewith my soule was sharply gryde,
   such woundes soone wexen wider.
                (89–96)

There is play upon the idea of "play" in line 92, but the line does not move us on to "glaunce"; so, too, with "glide" and "glyder." In Virgil's third eclogue, at the end of the song, when the judgment should be made, Palaemon, the judge, refuses to settle such a great dispute (*non nostrum inter vos tantas componere lites* [108]). Spenser's judge, Cuddie, declares that each has won and gives out equal prizes. Spenser has thus played on our knowledge of the intrinsic contentiousness in "alternating song" to emphasize harmony of theme and form.

The song of the Bonilasse is an example of what Thomas Rosenmeyer calls "the pure pastoral lyric," a lyric more form than matter.[21] This lyric, most common in the confident decade of the '90s, signals by its very shape, its brevity, its short lines, its often identifiable repeated chorus that, despite its content, its mode is light, musical entertainment. When the eclogue frame is removed, as, for example, in the August and April songs anthologized in *England's Helicon*, no longer can the reader depend for interest upon the complication of point of view a frame provides. Thus the virtuoso singing voice seizes attention with intricacies of verse and rhythm.

If we read the April eclogue as it appears in *England's Helicon*,[22] the poem is literally taken over by a strong and manipulative "I" voice. The poet, as both director and actor, involves the reader wholly and, by use of his "I" voice, creates an Elizabethan masque before our eyes. The actions, or the usual thin thread of narrative appropriate to a masque, are not described in any realistic or objective fashion, but the poet gives the feeling of a total event. In Virgil's Daphnis eclogue events are narrated as a chronological sequence in a closed system, delimited by the postures of Daphnis, Menalcas, and Mopsus. Not so here. The song begins with two stanzas, preparatory to the actual vision of Elisa, in which the poet builds feelings of anticipation:

Ye dayntye Nymphs, that in this blessed Brooke,
   doe bathe your brest,
Forsake your watry bowres, and hether looke,
   at my request:
And eke you Virgins, that on Parnasse dwell,

Whence floweth Helicon the learned well,
   Helpe me to blaze
   Her worthy praise,
Which in her sexe doth all excell.
                    (37–45)

The poet, as director, calls the cast together to praise a yet unseen goddess: "Hether looke, at my request . . . Helpe me to blaze." He then directs the reader's attention: "See, where she sits"; but there is also audience participation in this event, which expands the pastoral world to include the entire fictive poetic world.

The poet challenges, insists on response: "Tell me, have you seene her angelick face/ . . . can you well compare . . ./Where have you seene the like? . . ." (72). He then gives his own testimony, a now familiar version of the *topos*—the power and beauty of royal Elisa astonishes the gods:

I sawe Phoebus thrust out his golden hedde,
   upon her to gaze:
But when he sawe, how broade her beames did spredde,
   it did him amaze.
                    (73–76)

This pattern continues with the poet calling the actors to their places: "Shewe thy selfe Cynthia" (83), "Ye shepheards daughters . . . hye you there apace" (128), "Now ryse up Elisa" (145); directing the reader's attention to those who arrive of their own accord: "I see Calliope speede her to the place" (100); giving his own ceremonial and conventional testimony to Elisa's value: "To her will I offer a milkwhite Lamb" (96), "Wants not a fourth grace, to make the daunce even?" (113); and asking, not rhetorical questions, but open-ended ones that demand answers: "Bene they not Bay braunches?" (105), "Whither rennes this bevie of Ladies bright?" (118).

The poetic importance of this structure for pastoral is that, while it makes extraordinarily vivid, almost chaotic, the movement that defines the world, its confidence and spontaneity draw us in. Similarly, in Spenser's *Epithalamion*, because the poet addresses variously "ye learned sisters," "ye nymphes of Mulla," his bride ("Wake, now my love, awake"), and the merchants' daughters, we respond as though we are the expectant guests ourselves when he calls out: "Harke how the Minstrels gin to shrill aloud" (129). Director, actors, and audience have put on the same "garment" or guise, which sets them all in one world. The "I" voice comments from *within* the convention, and not, as we shall observe in the seventeenth century, with a sophisticated audience from an omniscient vantage *without*. When the narrator thanks the April maidens, are we not ready to step forward to receive our "damsines" with the rest?

> And if you come hether,
> When Damsines I gether,
> I will part them all you among.
> (151–53)

In his book *The Jonsonian Masque*, it is just this special appeal to the audience that Stephen Orgel takes as "the chief characteristic of the masque. . . . It attempted from the beginning to breach the barrier between spectators and actors, so that in effect the viewer became part of the spectacle. The end toward which the masque moved was to destroy any sense of theater and to include the whole court in the mimesis—in a sense, what the spectator watched he ultimately became."[23]

In contrast to the extroverted and exuberant mood of the April eclogue, the final lines of the December eclogue, with which the cycle closes, seem to turn the pastoral world in on itself, to close us inside the fold with the possibilities for our participation, to accuse us, in such questions as, "Ah who has wrought my Rosalind this spight / To spil the flowres, that should her girlond dight?" (114). And this is as it should be because we, like Colin, have seen the "yeare draw . . . to his latter terme" (127).

But with the final adieus of Colin, we do not put out the light on the pastoral world. In Virgil's ninth and tenth eclogues the beech tops are broken, the shades grow harmful to singers, and the poet separates himself from the dying pastoral world. Spenser's "shepheards' boyes" go on in merry glee; even Colin's own reed pipe is commended for its sound and hung upon a tree as a generous votive offering—not as symbol of the exhaustion of meaning in pastoral. And indeed, there is a repetition of the intimate tone we noted in the November eclogue when "Lobb" was assured that Dido's loss was joyful. Colin addresses a flock going off not to death but to the conventional protective place of the pastoral world:

> Gather ye together my little flocke,
> My little flock, that was to me so liefe:
> Let me, ah lette me in your folds ye lock,
> Ere the breme Winter breede you greater griefe.
> (145–48)

The December eclogue ends only one cycle of pastoral song, not all; Colin's meaning is not, finally, death, but termination. There is no paradox in his withdrawal, because it merely completes this cycle of nature, these landscape metaphors standing for these psychological moments of man; the poetry tells of this, as well as of death. Hobbinol's telling Rosalind "Adieu" will be continued in future pastoral verse.

CHAPTER 4

The Shepheardes Calender
in Religious and Political Perspective

A few days after her coronation service on January 15, 1559, at the ceremony for opening Parliament, Queen Elizabeth "rudely ordered the abbot and monks of Westminster to extinguish their ceremonial tapers. 'Away with those torches, we can see well enough!'"[1] The brilliance of the queen's choice of words illuminates the poise she established between ecclesiastical law and praxis, a poise that took into account the entire populace's nervousness about her religious position. While refusing to indulge in debate on such theological issues as whether there was a "real presence" in the Eucharist or the appropriateness of vestments, Elizabeth indicated that she would act on her sense of good politics for England.

"Away with those torches" might have been interpreted as a symbolic rejection, on principle, of all church accouterments, and would have signaled an improbable and incipient Puritanism on Elizabeth's part had it not been accompanied by the down-to-earth phrase "we can see well enough," which established a practicality fraught with meaning. It destroyed the possibility of rigid doctrinal interpretation, which the first phrase permitted, and became, instead, a statement about the quality of perception, an approach to theology rather than a prescription or a set of rules. In the phrase "see well enough," Elizabeth refers literally to the natural light of day, but her weightier meaning refers to the inner light, the more powerful and important kind of sight. Elizabeth thus underscores the insignificance of ceremonial conformity in contrast to the import of private godliness.

Whether it was a rationalization for responding first to the interests of the secular state and its precarious political position or an ideological commitment to individual freedom, Elizabeth's disavowal of her power over the inner life of her citizens profoundly affected the range of possible attitudes toward religion. Tudor historians Patrick Collinson[2] and A. G. Dickens agree that in the early Elizabethan church, perhaps because all non-Catholics had united in the severance from papal authority or because national unity seemed imminent, a loose consensus prevailed. Among Elizabeth's powerful bishops were former Marian exiles. The Calvinist notion of predestination joined "the two basic tenets of Protestantism—the unique and exclusive authority of the Scriptures and the sanctity of the human conscience in their interpretation."[3] In fact, Elizabeth's archbishop, Matthew Parker, had gone underground during the Marian persecutions; he was married, and had a reputation as a devoted reformer. The upheaval anticipated by the Catholics did not materialize. William Allen, an exiled Catholic who trained missionaries on the continent, stated it accurately. Of the government stand concerning the threatening Catholic factions he said, the government either admits that "our religion is true" or else that "they care not for it nor what we believe, no further than toucheth their prince and temporal weal."[4] The minimal prescriptions for conformity that Elizabeth imposed on the church suggest a political strategy and goal. National unity was not to be substituted for godliness, nor was private belief to be forced into the sphere of public conscience.

Elizabeth found support in an extensive but silent plurality of her subjects who, hungry for a respite from religious controversy that had forced them to please a succession of capricious monarchs, willingly embraced "a government which secured every man's life and property"[5] and freed them from death-dealing doctrinal disputes. Elizabeth had collaborators in her populace—stolid, peace-loving citizens. In *Tudor England*, S. T. Bindoff sums up the meaning of the Elizabethan church. It "was designed to appeal to the lukewarm multitude, and it enlisted their lukewarm support. To most members of Parliament, as to most Englishmen, its chief merits were negative. It had no Pope, it had no Mass, it made no windows into men's souls, it lit no fires to consume men's bodies."[6] In *The English Reformation* Dickens ventures further, suggesting that, at the time of Elizabeth's accession, many people actively welcomed the freedom to be indifferent to theological and doctrinal matters. The active reformers and "the exiles most under Genevan influence did not return in time to share in the political bargaining of 1559," but even when radical factions did attempt to make the church their forum, "the conservative tastes of the Queen, . . . erastianism, secularism, . . . the fear of disunity in the face of Spain and political Catholicism" checked "fissiparous tendencies within English Protestantism."[7]

Despite the minimal divisiveness at the time of the settlement, an honest assessment of Elizabeth's early years reveals not an absence of religious disputation, but a rigorous, sometimes passionate debate among intellectuals and elites within the church, the university, and the government. Between Elizabeth's coronation in 1559 and the publication of *The Shepheardes Calender* in 1579, when Spenser was in his late twenties, conflicting currents took form and sharpened the issues that were to divide Anglicans and Puritans—both were then unnamed reforming factions. Within the political structure of the church and within the universities particularly, certain issues born of the intellectual's critical consciousness and the churchman's vested interest in the established system or its overthrow clouded Elizabeth's horizon. Church historians locate the first explicit controversy in the decade of the '60s over a seemingly superficial issue—clerical vestments and liturgical ceremonies. The vestarian controversy erupted in the parliamentary convocation of 1563, where Puritans barely lost a vote on the imposition of a series of articles greatly at variance with the Ornaments Rubric of 1559.[8] The queen, dismayed by the laxity of worship she had seen in her progresses, had issued orders against clerical marriage, lectured her bishops on their responsibilities to force the clergy to wear proper vestments, and, in general, had indicated that she disliked the weakening of her political domination.

William P. Haugaard, whose book *Elizabeth and the English Reformation* explores primarily the 1563 convocation, concludes that angry militants in the lower house who opposed the queen had set the tone for the future. "Already the division between the bishops and the militant reformers was rapidly becoming wider than that between the bishops and the Queen."[9] Two years after the 1563 convocation, people continued to say their rosaries in corners and travel about without the distinguishing clerical vestments. A comment made by the moderate Bishop Alley reveals that the issue was not what one wore but the political implications of nonconformity: "It be all one in effect, to wear either round caps, square caps, or button caps, yet is thought very meet that we, being of one profession, and in one ministry, should not vary and jangle one against the other for matters indifferent; which are made politic by the prescribed order of the prince."[10]

In a letter to Archbishop Parker in 1565, Elizabeth wrote that she viewed the vestarian controversy as a measure of her failed power. Her phrases—"an open and manifest disorder," "diversity of opinions and specially in the external decent, and lawful rites and ceremonies," "such diversities varieties, novelties"—do not speak theologically of holy wrath and divine retribution at the Judgment Day.[11] The queen merely asserts that the conscientious exercise of power depends on a certain pedestrian orderliness in the social fabric. Elizabeth thus began to discipline recalcitrant clergy—and anger against her interference heightened. One loyal bishop wrote in 1573 "At the beginning it was but a cap, a surplice, and a tippet; now, it is grown to bishops, archbishops, and cathedral churches, to the overthrow of the established order, and to the Queen's authority in causes ecclesiastical."[12]

Spenser had been a student at Cambridge at least a year when, as though to mark the escalation in conflict and polarization, a political dismissal took place there. Although Thomas Cartwright had survived the vestarian controversy, when he spoke from the Chair of Divinity against the established church in 1570, William Cecil, the chancellor, first suspended and then dismissed him, at the end of that year, and he withdrew to Geneva. The occasion produced the "first great literary engagement between Anglicanism and Puritanism"[13] —between Vice-Chancellor Whitgift, the force behind the expulsion, and Cartwright.

Between evolving Puritan and Anglican factions, agreement prevailed on theological questions such as predestination, original sin, good works, and justification by faith—these were the givens of an English world view, as comments on the original articles of the settlement show. Even Whitgift "was a strict Calvinist, who upbraided Cartwright himself for venturing to say that the doctrine of free will was 'not repugnant to salvation.'"[14] But within this broad framework, Cartwright and the radical reformers saw unchallenged power exercised at the expense of simple people and simple issues. They thought the church both complacent and lax. The educational function of the church came under fire for perpetuating a clergy that was ignorant and unable to preach and for inflicting upon naive people a harmful prayer book of popish laws. But no less in question was the entire church structure, which delegated power from queen to archbishop to bishop; many reformers felt that power should arise from the people within each separate congregation through ministers of equal authority and with mutually imposed disciplines.

For Spenser, a young student at Cambridge (a university labeled a hotbed of Puritanism), the Whitgift-Cartwright debate must have been at least thought-provoking and, more probably, challenging in the most fundamental way. Although we lack a full text of the debates, Collinson believes that "their topicality aroused an enthusiastic response from the younger element in the university, and a marked reaction from the university authorities and the government which led to a 'hurly-burly and shameful broil' between two opposed factions, dividing the university between them and threatening to split the Church."[15] We derive Spenser's position from the religious eclogues.

A moderate Puritan, Spenser raises, in *The Shepheardes Calender*, as Cartwright did in the debates, broad moral issues that touch people's lives daily—the teaching function of the church, for example; its responsibility to demand exemplary behavior of its clergy; its tacit sanctioning of excess. He keeps to a minimum satire and criticism of specific personalities, laws, or systems of church governance. He is enough of a reformer to side against Elizabeth in the matter of Archbishop Grindal, whose argument with the queen took place in 1577, two years before the

publication of *The Calender* and a year after Spenser had received his
M.A. and left Cambridge for London.

Before exploring the group of religious eclogues, I discuss the issue
of Grindal—the Algrind of the May and July eclogues. In his approval of
Grindal, Spenser clarifies his own reformist tendencies, and suggests,
as well, that, in a healthy realm, the poet can both affirm the ruler's
beneficence and criticize her. (This is a point that becomes clear in retro-
spect when, in "Colin Clout's Come Home Againe," healthy criticism
from Spenser has been silenced.) My interpretation of Spenser's position
is not, however, universally shared. One critic, for example, does not
even entertain the idea that Spenser would contradict the queen. This
perspective is presented in *Spenser's Shepheardes Calender: A Study in
Elizabethan Allegory* by Paul McLane.[16]

In *The Shepheardes Calender*, Spenser's attention to Grindal is both
startling and revealing. In the May and July eclogues, he calls Grindal
"Algrind" and cites him, first as an authority for the principle that
clergy may not live as lay men do ("May," l. 75), then as an interpreter
of Moses' exemplary behavior, and, finally, as a moral exemplar himself
("July," ll. 157, 215). For contemporary readers we can confidently say
that Spenser's "Algrind" *was* Archbishop Grindal; he is the only person
so clearly named in the eclogues, with the exception of Queen Elizabeth.
Thus, we may well ask what Grindal represented to Spenser.

Grindal's appointment by Elizabeth was greeted enthusiastically by
protestant nobility and gentry. Collinson writes that even a puritan
clergyman "who deplored the high estate which an archbishop was
obliged to maintain, and despised the 'policy' which had made Grindal
a great lord, was prepared to believe that he would prove 'a Phoenix,'
uncontaminated and able to eschew lordliness and 'keep the gospel.'"[17]
Collinson continues, "Grindal contrived to preserve the public charac-
ter of a transparently good man. Not self-seeking by nature, as a bache-
lor he was relatively immune from economic pressures which gave many
of his fellow-bishops a mercenary reputation."[18] Even before his princi-
pled defiance of the queen, Grindal must have been a model to Spenser,
thoroughly admirable for finding an honorable way to live despite the
glitter and temptation of the Elizabethan church and court.

The incident to which Spenser refers at the end of the July eclogue—
the eagle dropping a shellfish on Algrind's head—concerned Grindal's
official disgrace and consequent deprivation. Grindal, who at Elizabeth's
accession had returned from exile in Strasbourg a Calvinist in theology,
disliked vestments and images, and was a proponent of prophesying. In
the past a tradition of Biblical interpretation conducted in Latin by
clergy, prophesying, under the reformer's church, became a means of
educating the laity. Conducted in English, these meetings or discussion

groups were discouraged by Elizabeth, who thought they engendered "religious novelty and subversive political opinions."[19] In 1576, when Spenser would have been writing *The Calender*, Grindal argued with Elizabeth over prophesying, offered to resign, and was, instead, suspended from ecclesiastical function for five years. To the queen he wrote impressively, "I cannot with safe conscience, and without offense to the majesty of God, give my consent to the suppressing of the said exercise; much less can I send out my injunction for the utter and universal subversion of the same . . . What should I win if I gained—I will not say a bishopric—but the whole world, and lose mine own soul?" He demands that Elizabeth leave religious questions to churchmen and attend to secular matters of the palace. Her overstepping of secular boundries ". . . is the antichristian voice of the Pope: 'So I will have it; so I command; let my will stand for a reason.'" Finally, he reminds her that "she is a 'mortal creature' with a 'corruptible body which must return to the earth, God knows how soon.'"[20]

McLane has difficulty explaining Spenser's sympathy with Grindal; he concludes that Spenser's "admiration [for Grindal] need not indicate complete correspondence in religious views or even agreement on the value of prophesyings."[21] He takes the classical libertarian view—Spenser sympathized with Grindal's "predicament" and "admired his character." However, this is simply not the case.

Spenser sympathized with Grindal, not for his principled stand, but because of the *principles for which he stood.* In telling us Grindal's interpretation of Moses' life in July, Spenser is both practicing and approving prophesying. Spenser certainly does not criticize Grindal either for accepting the bishopric *or* giving it up. The only lesson one could draw from July is that one risks more in high places. One might guess as well that the issue of teaching by example, leading the way to virtue, must have been close the poet's heart.

ii

Of the twelve poems of *The Shepheardes Calender*, three are in the tradition of religious satire (in which shepherd stands for pastor). This proportion indicates that man's experience of God has equal importance with his experience of love, mortality, and art. Just as Spenser teaches us personally to understand and reconcile ourselves to love pain, so he would teach us the proper public balance between pragmatism and principle, between the Elizabethan religious order and the ideas of the primitive church. In "May," "July," and "September," he portrays reality in commonplace satiric conventions: clergy, corrupted by money and power, live in a world of deceit, flattery, exploitation, and competition. Without moral exemplars, men strive, with a certain brutality, to enjoy the things of this world. The world is attractive, and there are attractive arguments to be made for embracing it; however, to establish an English *modus vivendi*, one begins not with debate over ceremonial tapers and the symbolism of the host but with the primitive or simple virtues—love, humility, social responsibility, generosity. The poet, himself a moral exemplar and teacher, works out a way to live virtuously in the contemporary world. His tone and language in these eclogues comes from homily.

Of the three eclogues, "May" presents the most coherent example of Spenser's homiletic technique. The frame of the poem sets out contradictory positions: that man should enjoy worldly pleasures God intended for him; that the world presents tinsel attractions that responsible people eschew. As does "May," "July" takes an argument that, initially, seems to pose a choice—the life of the low shepherd or the life of the hill-sitting goatherd—and develops the force of each alternative. This I have already discussed. September, the subject of much of the final section of this chapter, bears the burden of the critique of the clergy, corruption in the church hierarchy, and dissolute mores among the flock. In its fable, Spenser addresses the misuse of power and its consequences, the ways of deceit, and the unwillingness of man to be always vigilant.

In the May eclogue, following a Chaucerian spring opening, Piers and Palinode debate acceptable attitudes toward the things of this world. Piers calls Palinode a "worldes child" (73), preoccupied with the heritage he will heap up for his heirs instead of with the welfare of his flock. As illustration, he tells of an ape who embraced her "youngling" to death with a too-possessive love (100). In days when shepherds had neither "inheritaunce, land, nor fees" (105)—in other words, when people gathered food and there was no money economy—simple harmony with nature prevailed, each man free to take enough of honey, milk, and whey, none fearing for the precarious future. Palinode makes a strong argument against self-denial and for the inevitability of sorrow; pain and woe in the world need not be actively courted. Piers establishes his distrust of erring shepherds and, as illustration, tells the fable of the mother goat who, after leaving her kid with instructions against "treecheree," returns to find that he has been tricked and carried off by a fox disguised as a peddler of baubles. The brunt of criticism falls on the powerful fox, but the neglectful mother is not totally spared. Palinode praises the tale, but remains skeptical of Piers's argument. Shadows fall and the singers leave the stage.

"May" incorporates contradictions at the outset because it begins as a fresh, traditional *chanson de mai*:

> Is not thilke the mery moneth of May,
> When love lads masken in fresh aray?

How falles it then, we no merrier bene,
Ylike as others, girt in gawdy greene?
Our bloncket liveryes bene all to sadde,
For thilke same season, when all is ycladd
With pleasaunce: the grownd with grasse, the Woods
With greene leaves, the bushes with bloosming Buds.
                                                    (1-8)

It would take a particularly acute reader to predict from the plural
"*we* no merrier" that Spenser has transformed the common convention.
It usually goes: spring is the time for happy love; the unfulfilled lover is
sorrowful. Indeed, Palinode's observation that, while others bring in
May, he sits "drownd in a dreme" (16) suggest his failure against the
pure, godly festivity of those who gather "buskets" and smelling briar,
"dight the kirke pillours," and dance to the pipe. Only after 35 lines of
poetry does Palinode suggest another emphasis—that Piers might be envi-
ous of those who sport much and work little. Even then, we tend to
ignore this sour moralism, and to admire fetching home May, which
"acts out an experience of the relationship between vitality in people
and in Nature."[22]
     Piers then replies:

Perdie so farre am I from envie,
That their fondnesse inly I pitie.
Those faytours little regarden their charge,
While they letting their sheepe runne at large,
Passen their time, that should be sparely spent . . .
                                                    (37-41)

The game is up; we have easily assented to a pagan ritual and have ig-
nored the hints (plural "we"; much-sport-for-little-work) that all these
shepherds are pastors or religious leaders. Palinode is not a sorrowing
lover; he expresses a cosmic sorrow for the ways of the world. Spenser
has been using "Maying" charm to prepare us for the difficulty one
faces in measuring and evaluating one's social responsibility. As readers,
we have experienced the attraction of worldly pleasures that Piers would
discuss.
     But we are "men of the laye" (76). Spenser's true bitterness falls on
irresponsible shepherds who must protect and set an example for "the
bare sheep" (107). Palinode rebuts Piers's argument in standard though
somewhat illogical terms. We should not court sorrow; it will "come with-
out calling anone" (153). (Palinode assumes, one would guess, that living
as a moral example must be unpleasant.) The argument for clerical respon-
sibility appears more clearly in the fable of the fox and the kid.
     Problems of deceit, self-deception, and the distribution of social

responsibility tie the fable to the preceding section of the poem. If Piers's criticism weighs against worldly shepherds who spend their time in wanton merriment, then the mother goat plays the role of irresponsible pastor, her son, the exploited, innocent folk, and the fox, the potentate who bears more blame than the mother for corrupting the "Kiddie." The mother goat goes off to pursuits suspiciously like those of the May revelers at the opening of the poem. She "yode forth abroade unto the greene wood, /To brouze, or play, or what shee thought good" (178). The young son, in his fresh, blooming sexuality (which the mother charmingly appreciates—she "gan his newe budded beard to stroke" [214]) seems an appropriate figure for a flock in need of firm, vigilant guidance. Left without his mother, the kid is exploited by the deceitful fox, who should be the moral exemplar.

The fox does not simply trick the kid by the allure of the bells, babes, and glasses he carries in his peddler's pack. Spenser would portray the kid not as mindless, silly, and irresponsible like his mother but as naively good, in contrast to the fox, who is consciously evil. At the kid's door, the fox calls out blasphemously, "Jesus blesse that sweete face I espye" (256); he feigns mortal illness, claims kinship with the kid, and asks mercy and favor, the responses to which define one as Christian. The kid's goodness and simplicity bring his death.

In accord with the conventions of pastoral, the final lines of the eclogue, spoken in turn by Palinode and Piers, return the poem to the activity of singing. Also in accord with convention, Palinode attempts to reconcile the shepherds' divergent perspectives on worldly pleasure and responsibility by praising Piers's tale, even if he cannot accept the reforming intention of the singer. Palinode wants to borrow the tale "For our sir John, to say to morrowe/At the Kerke . . ./For well he meanes, but little can say" (309–11). But Palinode's pastoral gesture of acceptance also illustrates Piers's earlier assertion that the clergy are ignorant and irresponsible. Spenser's poetic harmony thus remains unconvincing. After the fable, the aphorism—"Let none mislike of that may not be mended" (162)—is unacceptable to readers of the eclogue.

iii

I have suggested that, by the late '70s, from robe and tippet, debate among intellectuals had broadened to episcopacy in church government and its inevitable reflections on the royal powers. The established church of which Elizabeth was supreme head had replaced papal jurisdiction with a hierarchical, centralized structure that "abounded with pluralities, sinecures, licences, dispensations, officials, fees."[23] Because its head was no longer a foreign pope, people could see close-at-hand its highly politicized officeholders. The political, worldly nature of the church tormented Puritans. Collinson confirms that, following Grindal's deprivation, there were ominous changes in Parliament. "If the disaster of Grindal was one token reaction, the changes that now took place in the composition of the episcopal bench were another. In the later 'seventies, the substance of power in the Church passed from the progressive bishops . . . into the hands of a new generation who were glad to adopt as their own the queen's view that the status quo must be strictly and equally maintained against both papists and puritans. . . . The indications are that the queen was now taking a more direct interest in bishop-making."[24] That fact in itself represented a strengthening of the hierarchical administration of power. The Puritan position, which was already being played out in Presbyterian Scotland, set church governance and discipline in the hands of congregation and ministers and, by a plea for broad dissemination of responsibilities, made a radical attack on hierarchical delegation of power.

Spenser's specific claims against the church are subordinate to his view that lordship, power, and money are not simply destructive, but, rather, are profoundly dehumanizing. While he provides a description and experience of clerical corruption, he does not prescribe a system of church governance or law. In the final section of this chapter, I give two significant examples of Spenser's indifference to law, and then go on to explore his interest in the alternative economic arrangements of the pure pastoral world as an ideal against which the failures of the present can be measured.

In the May eclogue, Spenser indicates that he would permit clerical marriage, but this is of passing interest. He wants to make the point that a good pastor would trust God to care for his offspring. The good pastor would not hoard wealth to pass on to his heirs.

> The sonne of his loines why should he regard
> To leave enriched with that he hath spard?
> Should not thilke God, that gave him that good,
> Eke cherish his child, if in his wayes he stood?
>   (83–86)

Similarly, in the matter of images and idols, Spenser's criticism disregards the link of objects with popery, despite a plank of the reformers' platform of the 1563 convocation: bishops and their officials were to search out "books, images, beads, and other superstitious ornaments used in time of papistry."[25] In the May eclogue, the fox is made to deceive the kid by playing on his narcissism. The fox wears "a trusse of tryfles at hys back" among which is a glass,

> Wherein while Kiddie unwares did looke,

He was so enamored with the newell,
That nought he deemed deare for the jewell . . .
(275-77)

He saves a bell in the basket, however:

Which when the Kidde stooped downe to catch,
He popt him in, and his basket did latch.
(289-90)

Surely, the objects stand for papist ornaments, but Spenser has no complaint against the material objects themselves. In the word "popt," he suggests the reckless way in which irresponsible clergy make people into valueless objects.

Even in the September eclogue (which, because of its specific language, we might expect to support particular laws or protest the absence of correct ones) the burden of criticism proceeds from observation of human behavior and a sense of disgust at the dehumanizing effect of gluttony, surfeit, and greed. Indeed, the imagery of a clergy metamorphosed into fattened bulls bursting their skins asks from the reader a visceral reaction of distaste, not an intellectual or legalistic one. The shepherds look "bigge as bulls that bene bate" (46), seem "beastly and blont" (109) (dull, clumsy), and their behavior is mild compared with that of the potentates in the hierarchy who are the real exploiters—some say "other the fat from their beards doen lick" (123). These "butten the more stoute" (125) with their hornes, while "treading leane soules" underfoot (126).[26]

In a simple golden world economy, the qualities needed by pastors can be those of shepherds—meekness, mildness, simplicity, humility, equality. In the golden world no hierarchy need develop in which certain people become moral exemplars to unshaped, slack psyches; rather, each man lives in an exemplary fashion.

The three religious eclogues present two sets of conventions—those that define the simple life and those that elaborate the falling off from virtue. In the May eclogue the golden age is defined by an absence of private property. Shepherds "had none inheritaunce/Ne of land, nor fee in sufferaunce" (105). Similarly, in "July," Abel's life of "little gayne" is exemplified by the sacrifice he performs on the altar—from his small store he gives a kid or sheep to God. Both Moses and Aaron conventionally seek, in the double sense of pastoral, neither to be "chiefe" nor to fall off from "simplesse." "September," which bears the weight of Spenser's specific criticisms of the clergy, introduces Roffynn the good shepherd—"with his worde his worke is convenable" (175). These define ideal or primitive pastoral.

The second set of conventions elaborates clerical corruption such as heaping up wealth for heirs ("May," 1. 92; "September," 1. 115), traveling to a far-off "place to seek wealth or unknowne gayne" ("September," 1. 72), robbing fellow shepherds ("September," 1. 36), profiting from the work of "leane soules" who are "treaden under foote" ("September," 1. 125), letting sheep lose their lustiness to become "sterved with pyne and penuree" ("September," ll. 63 ff.), and, perhaps most important, selling, buying, and killing flocks for gain ("May," ll. 47–50, 128; "September," 1. 39). Even the story of Roffy's battle against the marauding wolf in sheep's clothing, while it elaborates the many faces of deceit, stresses that greed and covetousness, not need, motivated the wolf "that with many a lambe had glutted his gulfe" (185).

Analysis of a passage from "September" demonstrates the thrust of Spenser's critique:

> Diggon
> In forrein costes, men sayd, was plentye:
> And so there is, but all of miserye.
> I dempt there much to have eeked my store,
> But such eeking hath made my hart sore.
> In tho countryes, whereas I have bene,
> No being for those, that truely mene,
> But for such, as of guile maken gayne,
> No such countrye, as there to remaine.
> They setten to sale their shops of shame,
> And maken a Mart of theyr good name.
> The shepherds there robben one another.
> And layen baytes to beguile her brother.
> Or they will buy his sheepe out of the cote,
> Or they will carven the shepherds throte.
> The shepherds swayne you cannot wel ken,
> But it be by his pryde, from other men:
> They looken bigge as Bulls, that bene bate,
> And bearen the cragge so stiffe and so state
> As cocke on his dunghill, crowing cranck.
>
> Hobbinoll
> Diggon, I am so stiffe, and so stanck,
> That uneth may I stand any more:
> And nowe the Westerne wind bloweth sore,
> That now is in his chiefe sovereigntee,
> Beating the withered leafe from the tree.
> Sitte we downe here under the hill:
> Tho we may talke, and tellen our fill,
> And make a mocke at the blustring blast.
> Now say on Diggon, what ever thou hast.
> (28–54)

Religious and agricultural worlds mesh. Thus, though Spenser echoes

Virgil, *Eclogue I*, in the conventional journey from the *locus amoenus* to "forrein costes," he does not emphasize the contrast between Rome that *inter caput extulit urbes* (24)—lifts its head among cities—and the country town, nor does he fix and describe geographical places. Absent also is the usual accompanying differentiation between public and private life. For Spenser, all geographical places are one; only moral landscapes vary, and these are characterized by the quality of daily life, a life neither public nor private but (and this is a different category), in this case, harsh, disonant, inhumane, deceitful, and poetically unlyrical. Such phrases as "of guile maken gayne," "setten to sale," "maken a Mart," and "layen baytes" describe a moral landscape in which men have been made objects of barter. Worldly pride had led Diggon to glorify the possibility of "eeking his store"; his sore heart, his misery, and his need to return home signal his healthy refusal to become the inhuman object of money.

Shakespeare understands this dehumanizing power of money and touches on it in the rustic pastoral of *As You Like It*. The shepherd Corin's human desire to offer hospitality to the weary travelers Rosalind and Celia is thwarted by the economic relations between him and his master. He says to Rosalind, who is disguised as a boy:

> Fair sir, I pity her
> And wish, for her sake more than for mine own,
> My fortunes were more able to relieve her;
> But I am shepherd to another man
> And do not shear the fleeces that I graze.
> My master is of churlish disposition
> And little recks to find the way to heaven
> By doing deeds of hospitality.
> Besides his cote, his flocks, and bounds of feed
> Are now on sale . . .
>
> (II, iv, 70–79)

When Karl Marx, using speeches of Shakespeare's Timon and Goethe's Mephistopheles as examples, calls money "the alienated power of humanity,"[27] he envisions such a scene. The shepherd Corin has been robbed of his power to respond to human need. Marx comments: "Money then appears as a disruptive power for the individual and for the social bonds, which claim to be self-subsistent entities. It changes fidelity into infidelity, love into hate, hate into love, virtue into vice."[28]

In the September eclogue Spenser juxtaposes to his vision of alienated humanity real relations in nature and human nature. It is not just the *succedimus antro* (let us go into the cave) convention that leads Hobbinol to invite Diggon "under the hill," but a recognition of his fundamental human need for shelter, a need which is further defined when, in Virgilian mood, he invites Diggon to lie in a "vetchy bed" at his cottage. September weather falls hard on the two shepherds, but they know themselves in it and protect each other. Similarly, in *As You Like It*, Duke Senior, without restrictive economic relations, responds to human need with extraordinary directness and simplicity, inviting Orlando to share his simple food. The vocabulary and syntax present human interaction free of mediating rhetorical figures:

Orlando: "I almost die for food, and let me have it."

Duke Senior: "Sit down and feed, and welcome to our table."
(II, vii, 104-5)

Though Orlando is anything by gentle, Duke Senior assumes that gentleness will be exchanged for gentleness. Marx helps again: "Let us assume man to be man, and his relation to the world to be a human one. Then love can only be exchanged for love, trust for trust . . . if you wish to influence other people you must be a person who really has a stimulating and encouraging effect upon others. Everyone of your relations to man and to nature must be a specific expression, corresponding to the object of your will, or your real individual life."[29]

In "September," Hobbinol, symbol of the contented mind weaned from wandering, knows who he is and what he is about. He is neither deceived nor self-deceiver. His advice to Diggon suggests again that one cannot live in the contemporary world as in an Eden of simple values, that being human in a complex society means setting flexible, humane standards. While Colin Clout, the ideal shepherd, carefully tends his flock, Hobbinol rests from *his* labors, expressing a kind of level-headed recognition of the importance of self-preservation:

Ah, Diggon, thilke same rule were too straight,
All the cold season to wach and waite.
We been of fleshe, men as other bee.
Why should we be bound to such miseree?
(236-39)

And, even more extraordinary, he refuses to be dehumanized in his relationships to others. To Diggon, beset by a fortune more fickle than his own, he expresses direct, genuine sympathy, a willingness to share—"as I can I will"—and a wish for the fair fortune of his friend:

But were Hobbinoll as God mought please,
Diggon should soone find favour and ease.
(252-53)

While Spenser lacks the acumen and clarity in the September eclogue to designate the *source* of exploitative human relations and to use pastoral conventions as brilliantly as Shakespeare does, his largeness of mind allows him to set forth Roffy, Colin, and Hobbinol as variations of the responsible shepherd/pastor, and to demonstrate that the psychological questions of how to live most interest him. Elizabeth's phrase "Away with those torches, we can see well enough" marries theory and praxis, as do the religious eclogues. The poems' realism defines goodness and moral virtue only in accord with the human, the humane, and the possible in a complex, intensely political society. Hobbinol's simple phrase "We bene of fleshe, men as other bee" (238) is not an apology for human fraility but a large and moving gesture of acceptance of himself and others.

The Shepheardes Calender came to life during a period of nascent religious and political controversy and, while nationalism born of the government's laissez-faire policy in religion prevailed among common people, the ruling elites and their reforming counterparts had begun what was to be a divisive and fiery debate. Spenser, at Cambridge during the Whitgift-Cartwright controversy, certainly made a choice not to set out the religious problems of *The Calender* according to current terms or to align himself dogmatically with the Geneva reformers. This choice I interpret as a positive one, one based on a skepticism of systems, rules, and laws and accepting of a continual, healthy tension in man's attempt to know a good life in God, in love, in friendship, and in death.

CHAPTER 5

"Unmasked" by Circumstance:
The Failure of Pastoral Convention in
"Colin Clout's Come Home Againe"

 When Colin Clout hangs up his pipe and locks his sheep in their fold against "breme Winter" at the end of the December eclogue of *The Shepheardes Calender*, his dramatic gesture signals not the exhaustion of a genre of pastoral (as in Virgil's final eclogues) but, rather, the completion of one cycle of pastoral song. Nevertheless, while Spenser devotes much of *The Faerie Queene* to explorations of pastoral attitudes, Colin Clout, the poet's pastoral self or "mask," appears only twice more in Spenser's work, and only once again in an eclogue. In Book VI, Canto X of *The Faerie Queene*, Calidore, the Knight of Courtesie, discovers Colin piping to ladies, graces, and his love. The pastoral vision so much embodies the pure pastoral idea rather than a dramatic event that it "vanishes all away" and is "cleane gone" when Calidore, the social man, steps forward. Spenser seems to signify, by the intimacy and private devotion of the vision set within the wider world of Book VI, his nostalgia for the past, permissable relation between poet, his beloved, and Gloriana. In *The Shepheardes Calender*, Spenser, as "her shepherds swayne" Colin, had blessed in poetry the union between himself as representative of the simple folk and the "goddesse plaine" who loved her people so well.[1] The grand vision of Book VI does not explore this symbolic personal relation further, but, rather, concerns itself with social institutions encountered in the world of everyday. However, in all of Spenser's work Colin does claim one poem for himself beyond *The Shepheardes Calender*.

In the eclogue "Colin Clout's Come Home Againe," which was written in the early 1590s and which narrates Spenser's journey from Ireland to England and "home againe," no grand vision of the social world mediates between singer and monarch. The paraphernalia of epic and romance disappears—the world of knights, squires, beasts, and lovely ladies—and we are left in touch with the singer at work. Once Colin's voice alone controls the pastoral song, as single voices controlled *The Shepheardes Calender*, one revelation of *this* poem is what we might

119

have deduced from the ephemeral vision of Colin in Book VI. The old relation between queen and poet, their proximity in the charmed circle of Mount Acidale and in the April eclogue, exists no longer.

At the heart of pastoral is the shepherd-singer who entices the sophisticated audience outside the poem to enter into the green world by harkening to his song. If, as singer, he appeals to the ear, as shepherd, particularly in the Renaissance with its Christian view, he evokes the image of representative man. The audience understands through its identity with him that human complexity can be put in revealingly simple guise. Speaking of the shepherd-singer, William Empson says, "You take a limited life and pretend it is the full and normal one, [thus indicating] that one must do this with all life, because the normal itself is limited."[2] This "trick" of pastoral gives the shepherd-singer the power to reduce disparity of rank and circumstance and to remind us of our common humanity. Early in Elizabeth's reign Spenser exploited this democratizing tendency of pastoral to the fullest. The shepherd-singer had the magical power to bring Eliza into the green world, to celebrate the bond between subject and queen. No courtier poet could call Elizabeth "my goddesse plaine/ . . . Albee forswonk and forswatt I am."[3] This freedom belongs to the poet who wears the pastoral mask.

The version of pastoral that "Colin Clout's Come Home Againe" presents is interesting because, while seeming to respect the characteristics of pastoral that I have sketched, it does not present a coherent pastoral world. In this lengthy autobiographical poem, pastoral convention itself is defeated by the poet's own complex and uncertain voice, which breaks through the pastoral mask, intruding upon the green world. Although the shepherd-singer Colin calls the "bleating flocks to rest" in the eclogue's final line, this traditional gesture of reconciliation does not convince us that poet has accepted either the limitations of the mode or of his own life.

The poet has grown older and the world has changed. Although unacknowledged in the poem, we hear bitter criticism of the realm from which Spenser has been excluded through his ten years' residence in Ireland and because of the literary and political movements of the decade. The poet is no longer *vates*, culture bearer, and public spokesman for Elizabeth's political poise. "Colin Clout" fails because Spenser writes the eclogue as if Colin were still representative man, as if the old trusting relation between queen and poet were intact. He cannot, however, consistently force the young man's literary genre, which depended on that relation to contain the mature man's altered circumstance. The poem does not present a range of generalized "attitudes" as do *The Shepheardes Calender* and *The Faerie Queene*; rather it narrates a contradictory, unhappy, and ultimately personal story.

The clash of pastoral attitude with personal life in "Colin Clout" is evident in two significant ways: first, throughout the poem (and, often, inappropriately) a real "I" emerges to challenge the poet's pastoral mask; and, second, nonliterary facts of the quality of life in Ireland and England contradict the "facts" of pastoral convention.[4] Irish landscapes only sometimes represent the old pastoral stance in which nature tells us what we are. Rather, we encounter the effects of Irish colonial struggle upon court and countryside. Spenser's pastoral place is protected by a garrison of soldiers rather than by Elizabeth's love. And, in England, the poet does not succeed at dissociating Eliza from her flawed court.

Spenser writes "Colin Clout" not as a twenty-five-year-old Cambridge student, an ingenuous participant in the current debates of his day, but as an experienced man in his forties with major works and years of tough government service behind him. He writes not in a new mode but in the old mode that he himself established by conceiving pastoral as a poet's "garment" and the simple singer as the figure for the complex man in *The Shepheardes Calender*. There is a phrase in "Colin Clout" that the reader might do well to keep in mind in order to have a feeling for the poem's tone of nostalgia, of resignation, of evasion. When Thestylis, one of the Irish rural rout, asks Colin, about three-fourths of the way through the poem, the "pivotal" question—Why did you ever leave "that happie place" (England) to return to Ireland's "barrein soyle?"—he adds a seemingly gratuitous remark that, in another poem, might only serve to heighten the drama of Colin's answer. Thestylis says, "Most wretched he, that is and cannot tell." The source of Spenser's wretchedness[5] lies in his exile from the queen and court and in his reluctance to make Ireland home, but these truths cannot be "told" directly, and certainly not in pastoral. The conventions of the mode do not permit Spenser to tell us convincingly *why* Colin Clout has come home.

Spenser begins "Colin Clout" by explicitly reminding his readers to link this new poem with *The Shepheardes Calender*. The new poem, however, has none of the confident and consistent conceptualization of *The Shepheardes Calender*. Nature is sometimes emblematic of a state, sometimes descriptive of a geographical place. The singer Colin does not maintain his role as the simple man who "knows." Spenser's own voice, coming directly out of his life situation, at points breaks through, particularly toward the end of the poem, and dominates the work, adding a note of personal perplexity that this poetry is unable to accommodate. Along with the inconsistencies of voice, there are conflicting visions of Ireland, England and the court—and of Spenser's own lot. Colin warns the Irish swains not to "abandon quiet home" in Ireland for that "lives painted bliss"; he glorifies and mythologizes the Irish landscape with its "cooly shade" and "greene alders," then he refers to his home as "that waste, where I was quite forgot," "this barrein soyle,/Where cold and care and penury do dwell." Similarly, Cynthia's beauty robs Colin of speech, but he is unable to explain why Corydon, the day's "hablest wit," receives only mean wages from her.

Of the court, there is little that is unfamiliar. If the defeat of the Spanish Armada was Elizabeth's greatest victory, the unity that war brought to the country had its wake in internal political and religious dissension. The queen was no longer likely to marry or bear an heir. Burghley was in his seventies, his succession in dispute between Robert Cecil, his son, and the queen's young favorite, Robert Devereaux, the earl of Essex, who had supporters enough to constitute a political constituency.[6] The jockeying for power in the "climb-fall court" was a testimony to the reality that Elizabeth's reign was coming to an end. Younger men than Spenser were at the top; when Ralegh visited Spenser at Kilcolman in 1589 the Shepherd of the Ocean himself, after seven years at court, had been banished in an incident that still remains a mystery.[7] Spenser refers to Ralegh's predicament early in "Colin Clout," saying the courtier sings of Cynthia's "great unkindnesse" and "usage hard." Indeed, there was no man with a more heightened flare for drama than Ralegh, who must have set Spenser's attention on the relation between the queen and her courtier-poets. Ralegh was probably "the best hated man of the world, in Court, city and country," and Stephen Greenblatt is correct in fixing the source of that hatred in Ralegh's proximity to the queen. Speaking of Spenser's portrayal of the pair in Book II of The Faerie Queene, he cites the "almost hysterical anguish of Timias when he is abandoned in anger by Belphoebe"; Greenblatt adds, "More than anyone of stature in the court, Ralegh was committed in his whole being to that strange, artificial, dangerous, and dreamlike world presided over by Gloriana, the world of adulation so intense that it still has power to shock us."[8] Spenser must have heard much from Ralegh that prefigured his own failure to gain the court favor he, too, so evidently desired.

Soon after Ralegh's visit to Kilcolman, Spenser sailed with him to England, presumably bearing to the printer Ponsonby the manuscript of the first three books of The Faerie Queene. Of his activities while in England, we know little except that, having received a disappointing pension of £50, he returned to his estate in Ireland in 1591 to write "Colin Clout's Come Home Againe," the "Epithalamion," "Prothalamion," and Books IV–VI of The Faerie Queene. "Colin Clout," which he called "a simple pastorall . . . agreeing with the truth in circumstance and matter," he dedicated to Ralegh. Hardly sanguine in tone, his dedicatory note, printed with the poem, begs Ralegh to use his "good countenance . . .

against the malice of evill mouthes, which are alwaies wide open to carpe at and misconstrue my simple meaning." He signs himself "From my house of Kilcolman the 27. of December. 1591."

The quality of life in Ireland in the 1580s and '90s has been virtually ignored by readers of Spenser even though it is important to Book V of *The Faerie Queene* and essential to understanding the tensions and contradictions of "Colin Clout." Thomas Edwards, in an intelligent essay on "Colin Clout" (which I discuss later in detail), pins his analysis of the cumulative meaning of the poem on English facts, on court as the single *locus* of the meaning of the poem.[9] Thus he cannot imagine Spenser leading a full, complex life in Ireland knowing that country for itself and not simply as the place that "is not England." C. S. Lewis, in a brief comment on the poem, turns all attention to conflicts between the idea of Elizabeth's court and its reality. Calling "Colin Clout" "the most familiar and autobiographical of Spenser's poem," Lewis concludes that England's conditions make Ireland desirable, full of consolations. But Lewis, too, ignores the difference between "not being in England" and "being in Ireland":

> On the one hand, England is a paradise governed by a goddess, and the court a constellation of excellent poets and bright nymphs; on the other, that same court is a den of false loves, backbiting and intrigue, no place for any gentle wit, from which Colin chose 'back to his sheep to tourne.' This is very natural. Thus many an exile feels when he comes back . . . to his post after the longed for, the exciting, yet ultimately disappointing holiday in England. Doubly disappointing, because he has failed to get the job in England that he hoped for, and also wonders whether there are not, after all, many consolations for living abroad. I think that with Spenser these consolations were now more valuable than he fully realized, for though the poem contains bitter lines, the prevailing air is one of cheerfulness.[10]

If in Elizabeth's court Spenser was a powerless man, in Ireland he represented the crown and its power in a nation engaged in resistance to colonization. Indeed, in the early 1580s, Spenser carried out Lord Grey's policy of absolute suppression and, as private secretary to that crusading zealot, must have accompanied Grey as he used his sword to put down the Catholic rebels. By the time "Colin Clout" was composed, Spenser and Ralegh both had been some years in "planting" the colony of Munster, a process by which each county was divided up and given over to English landlords who were to bring the rebels who lived on the land under control.[11] Spenser, then, in both his public and personal life, played out the drama of the crown official, protecting himself, his property, and, later, his family, from attack and, in the process, experiencing the dilemma of any colonizer for whom liberal tolerance is a luxury afforded only to those at home. This rôle colors the imaginative landscape of "Colin Clout," forcing Spenser to recognize, as a secure landowner in England might not, that woods, field, and stream are of economic and political value before they are poets' idealized or emblematic forms. For the poet for whom a green shade had earlier been called a state of mind,[12] how ironic to make ownership and defense of property the condition for poetic tranquility.

Historians agree that the problem of land tenure in Ireland arose because the idea of property rights, the private holding of lands, was imposed on the Irish by their English rulers. The concept of private ownership was foreign to all Irishmen except those who were linked to England or the Continent by birth, wealth, or education. Early in his reign Henry VIII forced the powerful Irish chiefs to surrender their lands to him so he could regrant them in the name of the crown. In keeping with medieval tradition, the chiefs would be his fiefs. Henry, however, either explicitly ignored or simply did not recognize that land tenure in Ireland prior to his reign had followed a pattern foreign to English practice over the preceding few centuries.

The imposition of an English system was not only ill-advised, it was disastrous. A. L. Rowse, a historian who justifies the expansion of Elizabethan England, calls the land regrant system "a fundamental misconception which became one of the deepest sources of trouble for the next century. . . . English law simply could not define the situation in its own terms. . . . As time went on, this produced a fearful harvest of misunderstanding, mutual accusations and betrayals. For the chiefs could not deliver the goods: they depended for their position on the good-will of their [clans or] septs—there was the real source of their strength. But the septs understood very well what was the effect of granting away their lands."[13] Relations between English and Irish, between septs, chiefs, and English governors were necessarily ridden with conflict. Furthermore, in destroying the Irish system of tannistry (the term for the native land-holding system), the English did not substitute their own system of inheritance. Rather, royal prerogative designated ownership and succession into English hands, so that, at the owner's death, land reverted to the crown. This was the system of the Munster Plantation in which Spenser was a colonist; this also was the system in the Virginia Plantation in North America established in the same decade.

By the late Elizabethan age, when Sir John Davies, Celtic poet and statesman, wrote his tract *Discovery of the True Causes why Ireland was never entirely subdued nor brought under Obedience of the Crown of England*, he, along with others, had recognized the failure in intelligence and even in expediency in setting Irish policy:

If the Irish be not permitted to purchase estates of freeholds or inheritance, which might descend to their children, according to the course of our Common Law, must they not continue their custom of tannistry, which makes all their possessions uncertain, and brings confusion, barbarism and incivility? In a word, if the English would neither in peace govern them by the law, nor could in war root them out by the sword, must not they need be pricks in their eyes and thorns in their sides till the world's end, and so the conquest never be brought to perfection.[14]

This is the atmosphere of barbarism and incivility in which Spenser lived for almost fifteen years. Passages from Spenser's "A View of the Present State of Ireland," though less critical of the English than Davies' tract, pose a similar choice—continued defiance by the Irish in the face of tolerant reform or complete subjection and the establishment of English law throughout the realm. One should remember that Spenser does not describe "troubles," and impending "Rebellion" from the safety of England:

> ... everye daie we perceave the trowbles growinge more uppon us, and one evill growinge on another, in soe muche as theare is no parte now sounde or ascerteined, but all have theire eares uprighte waytinge when the watche worde shall Come That they shoulde all ryse generallye into Rebellion and Caste awaye the Englishe subjeccion ... and therefore where ye thinke that good and sounde lawes mighte amende and reforme thinges theare amisse, ye thinke surelie amisse. For it is vaine to prescribe lawes wheare no man carethe for kepinge them nor fearethe the daunger for breakinge them. But all the Realme is firste to be reformed and lawes are afterwardes to be made for kepinge."[15]

To his credit, Spenser had suggested earlier in the tract that small nations should have "lawes ... fashioned unto the manner and condycion of the people to whom they are meant,"[16] that English law ought not to have been imposed on Ireland. But his theoretical sense of justice found counterargument in daily necessity. Those "eares ... wayting the watch word" indicate that the Irish had little to lose by fighting. This pattern of conflict between idea and reality is repeated over and over in "Colin Clout."

Outside his castle at Kilcolman barbarous outlaws did threaten violence and, indeed, in 1597, Spenser's estate was sacked and Kilcolman burnt to the ground. In the final lines of "A View," he commends "matchavell" for noting a Roman policy of giving absolute power and the responsibility therefore to provincial or colonial governors and consuls, for these officials of the crown must rule with a ruthlessness unbecoming most monarchs.

If social and economic conditions impinging upon Spenser' life in England and Ireland provide the backdrop for "Colin Clout," eclogue supplies the form into which these conditions are "fit." Indeed, the form was the logical choice, given the country-court journey, the single controlling voice, the friendship between men, and the comparison of values; this is the pastoral material of *The Shepheards Calender*, which Spenser had "translated" into its Renaissance form from its Virgilian origin, the material for which he became the authority. According to the convention of the '80s and '90s, a model poem for Spenser's journey would describe the poet-shepherd, guided by his companion singer (Ralegh), departing for court seeking knowledge and recognition, leaving the simple, sometimes troublesome rusticity of home. He has, in his mind's eye, an idealized place, which he has glorified from afar. Made aware of his naiveté by the decadence of court, by flattery, lies, backbiting, and the distressing way in which he is used, he comes to value himself newly for this very naiveté. At home again, his view has become complex, for he now holds simultaneously in his mind his original vision, which he cannot give up, and the disillusioned vision, which compares the court unfavorably with his native place. He is thus saddened, wiser, knows good by having met evil, and has deliberately chosen "his own lyfes estate." He is superior to us but, through him, we learn quite naturally to love what is complex because it is in simple guise.

"Colin Clout" fits this description and, indeed, some critics have interpreted it according to this model.[17] This model is, however, only partial, for embedded in the model and ultimately undercutting it is a second poem, which consists of Spenser's unsuccessful attempts to absorb into the happy formula his personal experience and the contingencies of an individual historical moment. Spenser, as Colin, makes a literal journey and speaks about it directly in his own voice. These distinctions are critical and must be kept in mind. In other journey poems of *The Shepheardes Calender*—"September," for example—the journey in space is simply a metaphor creating "distance" between possible lives. In Virgil's eclogues Rome, as a reality, remains obscure, a vague vocabulary beyond the world of the poem, and Tityrus' home is as different from the world beyond the farm as the eye of the hurricane from swirl of winds about it. Melibee, the old shepherd of Book VI of *The Faerie Queene* whose journey is most like that described in the model poem above, turns out to be an "attitude" rather than a character who goes anywhere at all.[18] Having left the pastoral place in his youth, Melibee returns home from court to assert familiarly:

> I from thenceforth have learn'd to love more deare
> This lowly quiet life, which I inherit here.
>
> (VI, ix, 25)

But Spenser's object in his portrait of Melibee is not to make a positive judgment about the shepherd's choice of a "lowly quiet life" over court pleasures. The key phrase is not "lowly quiet life" but "learn'd to love"; the well-known exchange between Calidore and Melibee explores in pastoral terms the commonplace—"it is the mynd that maketh good or ill." It matters little where one lives, as long as one accepts one's fortune with contentment.[19] Spenser illuminates the qualities of pastoral contemplation and heroic action, the strengths and self-knowledge drawn from each, and the power granted when one knows he can "fashion his own lyfes estate." The grandeur of Spenser's generalizations contradict and overshadow the particular facts of any single character's life. Indeed, such moments do make us want to name Spenser the poet without a self, for, if he feels less than accepting of his own life's estate, the poem gives no hint. This is Spenser's usual mode.

The "Prothalamion," small in form, like eclogue, and controlled by a single voice, provides a second point of comparison. It does accommodate some personal facts, but only by way of Spenser's announcing—in accord with acceptance of circumstance—that he chooses to celebrate and idealize another's love and marriage and put his own discontent aside. The opening verse sets the poet's "sullein care," "idle hopes," and "expectation vayne" against the wedding landscape, which has power to "ease his payne." By the eighth verse of the poem, when the complaining "I" is again heard, the potential for unattractive self-indulgence has been transmuted into a magnificent Spenserian moment in which the inclusion of the autobiographical "I" simply illustrates the appropriateness of transcending that "I." Personal woes are dismissed with the phrase "But Ah here fits not well/Olde woes but Joyes to tell." This denial, which, in fact, does tell woes, solves the problem causing "Colin Clout's" failure. Spenser affirms and celebrates good qualities in human nature—love, truthfulness, courage in the face of disappointment—while indicating simultaneously that his life and all lives must, in part, deny them.[20]

Melibee's journey turns out to be an "attitude," not a biography, while the autobiographical "I" of the "Prothalamion" could, most properly, be called a foil for presenting "Joyes." Only in "Colin Clout" must we account directly for the poet's real self and for a literal journey that precedes the poem and provides a backbone for it, a journey that is fact before it is metaphor.

ii

The first movement of "Colin Clout" (lines 1–155 of the 950 lines) follows eclogue tradition and establishes our expectation of conventional pastoral entertainment as developed by our model. A narrator sets the scene in which one shepherd, Hobbinol, questions another, Colin, about

his recent journey, using an elaborate representation of the mourning
of nature in his absence to request an account of that journey. A third
shepherd, Cuddy, interrupts Colin's story with a gracious request that
he sing the song he mentions in the beginning of his account. Colin ac-
cedes with the "ancient truth" of Old Mole, Mulla, and her brother-
lover Bregog. Further, he establishes his link not only with the history
of pastoral (Virgil's *Eclogues III* and *VI*, particularly) but with his own
accepted place as poet in that tradition. The reader is at home in a com-
fortable world where song has power to transform reality.

   If there is any "individuality" in this beginning, it is expressed in
the poet's authoritative voice in the opening lines, which echo and
transform the apologetic first lines of *The Shepheardes Calender*:

>   A shepheards boye (no better doe him call)
>   When Winters wastful spight was almost spent . . .
>   (*Shepheardes Calender*)

>   The shepheardes boy (best knowen by that name)
>   That after Tityrus first sung his lay . . .
>   ("Colin Clout")

Indefinite "a" changes to definite "the" and "no better" to "best know-
en";[21] Spenser directly claims his place as Virgil's successor by using
Virgil's commonly accepted pastoral name, "Tityrus." The shepherd's
boy of *The Calender*, although he presents himself as aging in the De-
cember eclogue and remembers his youthful time in "June," consis-
tently maintains the modest tone appropriate to eclogue as a young
man's form. The new Colin presents himself as an accomplished singer
whose reputation assures respect. He charms the

>   . . . shepheard swaines that did about him play;
>   who all the while with greedie listfull eares,
>   Did stand astonisht at his curious skill,
>   like hartlesse deare, dismayd with thunders sound . . .
>   (6–9)

Indeed, while "hartlesse deare" comes easily from the vocabulary of
love poetry, the words "astonisht," "dismayd," and "thunders sound,"
particularly in this order, have epic weight; Spenser has given us the
etymological meaning of "astonisht" (*tonare*, to thunder) by linking it
to "thunders sound." But shepherds, too, can become mature, and the
tone suits our knowledge of the autobiographical nature of the poem—
Colin is Spenser's pastoral mask.

   It is from such authoritative moments in the poem that Thomas Ed-
wards writes of "Colin Clout": "The pastoral frame brings with it the

idea of an art of moral innocence, a skilled simplicity that can look at
sophistication without being caught by its ironies and evasions."[22] Ed-
ward's analysis, which acknowledges the complexities of the poem and
the terms of Renaissance pastoral, shows just the problem that good
readers of pastoral may fall into. Utilizing his understanding of the Emp-
sonian notion of the "double" nature of pastoral, Edwards seizes on the
old pun on "feign" and "fain" and uses it to explain that "Colin Clout"
fulfills the central Virgilian eclogue sentiment that song, "short time[s]
endlesse moniment," is itself the *consolatio*, an invention that reconciles
the poet to failed preferment and ill-requited love:

> The old pun on 'feign' and 'fain' is relevant here: to desire someone or some-
> thing leads to pretending, inventing qualities in the other before they can be
> determined in fact, inventing a self who cherishes those qualities even though
> other people see through them, and finally inventing substitutes for the object—
> false memories, impossible futures—when it is absent or lost. . . . The point is
> that for both Spenser and Ralegh, the poet as reluctant recluse and the poet as
> unemployed soldier-politician, art is a response to banishment and a way,
> through feigned re-creation of distant objects of desire, to make banishment
> endurable or even 'mery.'[23]

Although it is not a misplaced critical observation to call failure one great
subject of art, Edwards' application of that observation to "Colin Clout"
is neater than the poem itself. The poem is already so wedded to longstand-
ing fact that neither desire nor invention can transmute palpable failure
into art.

The opening lines of the poem show what will become a pattern of
consistent intrusion by facts or what I call "life experience," which is
not transformed into art. Hobbinol asks Colin to tell the story of his
voyage, a standard opening to a court-country comparison. He uses the
word "voyage," not "journey," and this word choice underscores the
connection between the literal trip by sea and poetic convention. Hob-
binol's question is reversed syntactically, with the subordinate subjunc-
tive clause receiving emphasis at the head of the question:

> But were it not too painfull to repeat
> The passed fortune, which to thee befell
> In thy late voyage, we would thee entreat . . .
> (32–34)

While Hobbinol, true to pastoral manners, may simply be apologizing for
his request by acknowledging that singing takes work and is painful or la-
borious (thus reminding us to be appreciative listeners), the word "pain-
full" has more resonance than he can know. The word arises from the dis-
appointment of Spenser (not Colin) that England has been distressful to
the man and the poet, facts that the rural rout could not yet know. Fur-
ther evidence that "painfull" is a lapse in the pastoral mask comes in
Colin's answer. He ignores or evades Hobbinol's "painfull" and rather con-

ventionally embellishes upon the theme of his covetousness to discuss
"good passed newly" and his bliss at having seen "that Angels blessed eie."

A second song request comes from Cuddy some fifty lines later. He
asks for the song Colin sang for the Shepherd of the Ocean, Ralegh; ac-
cording to Virgilian convention, Cuddy suggests the standard genres:

> And should it not thy readie course restraine,
> I would request thee Colin, for my sake,
> To tell what thou didst sing, when he did plaie.
> For well I weene it worth recounting was,
> Whether it were some hymne, or morall laie,
> Or carol made to praise thy loved lasse.
>
> (82–87)

Colin, like Virgil's Mopsus, ignores these genres but connects his answer
to Cuddy's final phrase. Interestingly, he transmutes the impersonal
"loved *lasse*" into the private world of his own "love" and "*losse*,"
about which he refuses to sing. He will, instead, mythologize Irish land-
scape.

> Nor of my love, nor of my losse (quoth he)
> I then did sing, as then occasion fell;
> For love had me forlorne, forlorne of me,
> That made me in that desart chose to dwell.
> But of my river Bregogs love I soong . . .
>
> (88–92)

Colin leads us into a tantalizing realm of unspoken personal pain and
out again. Of whose love does he refuse to speak? Rosalind's? Eliza-
beth's? Is the equation "me forlorne, forlorne of me" a periphrasis hid-
ing Spenser's bitterness at his treatment by Elizabeth, as his claim to
self-chosen exile in the "desart" might suggest? We cannot know, nor
does the poem tell us how to reconcile this view of Ireland as a "desart"
with the initial pastoral portrayal.

The song of "my Bregog," however, is neat, contained, and altogeth-
er an appropriate pastoral entertainment. As a mythologizing of Spen-
ser's landscape it is "true" and important; Spenser and Ralegh meet at
the foot of Old Mole, the mountain that figures as father of Bregog's be-
loved Mulla. But, coming after Colin's explicit refusal of the personal,
the reader wants to evaluate the song for its meaning to the forlorn men
rather than for the singer's skill or art in accord with Virgilian pastoral
convention. Thomas Edwards finds one meaning. He shows that, even
though Old Mole thwarts Mulla's love, "Bregog's love is not just a past
emotion but a continuing one, despite the fact that the story ends with
Mole scattering Bregog's streams."[24] The crucial lines appear at the outset:

> But of my river Bregogs love I soong,

Which to the shiny Mulla he did beare,
And yet doth beare, and ever will, so long
As water doth within his bancks appeare.
(92–95)

Bregog's love, Edwards suggests, is like Spenser's and Ralegh's; Ralegh's own "lamentable lay" follows just after. Both men must transform rejection by the beloved into serene and continuing devotion that asks nothing in return; individual disappointment becomes the wellspring of art.

But Edwards' comparison between the two men and Bregog is faulty. Bregog and Mulla are star-crossed lovers of folklore, for she is quite as willing as he to follow him and her own heart rather than her father's authority. Spenser writes in a storytelling mode and approves her loyalty with an aphorism:

Nath lesse the Nymph her former liking held;
For love will not be drawne, but must be ledde,
And Bregog did so well her fancie weld,
That her good will he got her first to wedde.
(128–31) (Emphasis added.)

No deeper meaning emerges; Thestylis correctly pronounces himself entertained by the "mery lay."[25]

Even more significant, Edwards ignores the radical change in tone from Bregog's tale to Ralegh's "lamentable lay." Here are true moral and linguistic complexity:

His song was all a lamentable lay,
Of great unkindnesse, and of usage hard,
Of Cynthia the Ladie of the sea
Which from her presence faultlesse him debard.
And ever and anon with singults rife,
He cryed out, to make his undersong
Ah my loves queene, and goddesse of my life,
Who shall me pittie, when thou doest me wrong?
(164–72)

Bregog springs from mythic metamorphosis, the lay from a life. If Ralegh has been singing to Colin his "The Ocean to Cynthia," as critics suggest,[26] what Colin has heard is the death of meaning in Ralegh's world with the death of Elizabeth's love—not true lovers thwarted but the personal drama of a single lover living in "aching loneliness and the total isolation of the self."[27] The undersong says Elizabeth's is the only "pittie" in the world, and that world ceases to pity Ocean. Furthermore, the line "Which from her presence faultlesse him debard" permits the reader to hear "faultlesse" as ambiguous, modifying both "her" and "him." Colin thus sets Ralegh and the queen in a perplexing moral universe. The point of Colin's description is not, as Edwards suggests, to show steadfast devotion, but, rather to express pain and helplessness.

When, several lines later, Colin reports that the shepherd of the ocean bemoans Colin's "lucklesse lot," calls Colin a "wight forlore," "banisht" into a "waste unmeet for man," and urges him to "wend" to see Cynthia, we understand the personal identity between the two men. Spenser has used Ralegh's lot as a way of speaking of himself. In Ralegh's lay is Spenser's unspoken love and loss, all that cannot be told. These intrusions contrast with Bregog's story, which, in the end, we should evaluate as a skillful pastoral song. We can link it to Ralegh's ditty only by saying that the world of "Colin Clout" is inhospitable to lovers.

iii

The second movement of the poem (lines 178–358) takes the singers over the sea to court, where Ralegh introduces Spenser to "that Godesse grace." On the voyage the singer's story, like the tale of Bregog, does coincide with convention. The passage is perhaps the most coherent in the poem. The poet maintains his mask because the subject is pastoral friendship rather than personal pain. Colin flatteringly depicts Ralegh as Elizabeth's deputy on the ocean, then reports his naive response to the sea—it is "horrible," "hideous," and "roaring." Turning to Ralegh, his guide and sponsor, he makes known his "inwarde feare" and asks "under what skie, or in what world" he is. Ralegh translates ocean into countryside. He calls the Lady of the Sea a shepherdess and the "thousand fishes with their frie" flocks and herds. Transformed by Ralegh, the sea subsides from "a way leading down to hell" into a workaday water world where Triton has fish going "to and fro at evening and at morne."

As soon as they reach land Ralegh disappears and Cuddy takes up Colin's former conventional role as the naive one. He asks the classic eclogue question, with which the country-court contrast of the poem might be said properly to begin:

> What land is that thou meanst (then Cuddy sayd)
> And is there other, then whereon we stand?
> (290–91)

The reader expects the major comparison of the poem. The questioner's world should be compared with the world at the journey's end—either England's purity versus Ireland's decadence or vice versa. That expectation is defeated, this time not by the simple intrusion of an inappropriate word or phrase but by a lengthy passage that describes a rural life disrupted by political circumstance beyond the poet's control—what I call the real, material conditions that the poet does not turn into art.

Colin begins his answer to Cuddy by describing an Edenic England of "fruitful corn," "faire trees," and "fresh herbage." He likens Elizabeth to "lillies," "roses," "goolds," and "daffadilies." This is the flourishing world about which the new arrival should and does express admiration. However, instead of filling out the comparison between "there" (England) and "here" (Ireland) with a rustic pastoral to parallel the golden one, Spenser abandons the mythic world of Mulla, Bregog, and Old Mole, and confirms Ireland as an actual "waste" or desert.

> Both heaven and heavenly graces do much more
> (Quoth he) abound in that same land, then this.
> For there all happie peace and plenteous store
> Conspire in one to make contented blisse:
> No wayling there nor wretchednesse is heard,
> No bloodie issues nor no leprosies,
> No griesly famine, nor no raging sweard,
> No nightly bodrags, nor no hue and cries;
> The shepheards there abroad may safely lie,
> On hills and downes, withouten dread or daunger:
> No ravenous wolves the good mans hope destroy,
> Nor outlawes fell affray the forest raunger.
> There learned arts do florish in great honor,
> And Poets wits are had in peerlesse price:
> Religion hath lay powre to rest upon her,
> Advancing vertue and suppressing vice.
> For end, all good, all grace there freely growes,
> Had people grace it gratefully to use:
> For God his gifts there plenteously bestowes,
> But gracelesse men them greatly do abuse.
>
> (308-27)

His grim view of Ireland is set in a passage that uses England as its frame of reference. The list of what does not exist in England accentuates the clash of literary pastoral with social conditions. England has been so idealized in the preceding passage that we are jarred to hear "no wayling there" (in England), no "bloodie issues," "leprosies," "griesly famine," "ranging sweard," "nightly bodrags" (raids), "outlawes," "wolves," and so on. These signs of war and civil strife simply do not belong to the poem, even if they are intended to characterize Ireland. What is wanted for the comparison is "hard" or rustic pastoral, not the landowner's or government servant's account.

A View of the Present State of Ireland paints the same picture of Ireland and replicates the vocabulary of our list. In the best known

passage of the tract, Spenser portrays the beaten Irish brought to
"wretchedness" by the wars of Grey in Munster. Here are the results of
the "raging sweard" and "griesly famine." "Out of everie Corner of the
woodes & glennes they came crepinge forth upon their handes, for their
legges could not beare them, they looked Anatomies of Death, they
spake like *ghostes crying* out of theire graves, they did eate of the dead
Carrions . . . there perished not manye by the sworde, but all by the ex-
tremitye of *famyne*, which they themselves had wroght."[28] In a second
passage we learn what real dangers remain in the woods for shepherd
and forester. Spenser says he would forbid the wearing of mantles; the
garment "is a fitt house for an *outlawe*, a meet bedd for a *rebell*, and an
apte cloak for a *thief*, these when he flyeth from his foe and lurketh in
the thycke woodes and streight passages, waytinge for advantages, yt is
his bedd, yea and almost all his howshould stuffe; For the wood is his
howse against all weathers, and his mantle is his cave to slepe in . . .
when he goeth abroad in the *night* on *freebootinge*, yt is his best and
surest freind"[29] (emphasis added).

Then, following the section comparing Ireland and England (with
its subsequent praise of Eliza), Spenser for the first time directly under-
cuts England's virtues, and the English court appears conflictingly in
both its idealized and real lights. The bitterness against Irish reality and
the disillusionment with the uses of English bounty now leave little
"space" for pastoral solace. Although Ireland's pastoral potentiality
finds full expression in the final lines of the poem, Colin sings Ireland's
poetic praise long after we can believe in it.

The intruding lines do not tarnish the glorious praises of Cynthia
(which precede the passage and follow immediately after), but Colin
uses a *judgmental* tone that, more and more, will take over the poem.
"There" is England.

> For end, all good, all grace there freely growes,
> Had people grace it gratefully to use;
> For God his gifts there plenteously bestowes,
> But gracelesse men them greatly do abuse.
> (324-27)

The implication is that the singer is not one of those "gracelesse men,"
that he believes himself both graceful (with its meaning close to that
of "grateful") and morally superior. Although England may be literally
safe, free from the threat of murder ever present in "gracelesse" Ireland,
England holds no promise of moral safety. As private poet and mature
man he can define "grace"; he will not be the public voice for this
civilized world, which, in his judgment, has repudiated God's bounty.

Having undercut England, Spenser must attempt the impossible—to dissociate Elizabeth from her flawed court. His pastoral depends on the continued relation between low and high, singer and queen. The result is, first, evasion and, finally, stilted formulaic poetry. The third movement of the poem (ll. 358-771) begins with the standard question about the state of poetry at court. Some lines, while praising specific poets, describe the politics of preferment and indict the distribution of rewards. But complaints of penury, ill-favor, and injustice to poets are standard fare. What makes treatment of the *topos* complex and puzzling in "Colin Clout" is the fact that, because Spenser is no longer a confident critic, an insider, he attempts to criticize while giving the illusion of praise. The result is confusing specificity rather than the usual direct but general rebuke.

The October eclogue of *The Shepheardes Calender* is a useful point of reference. It mirrors the common Elizabethan belief about poets and poetry. In the golden world, in the Greco-Roman past, poets had true honor and honorable subject matter. Their lot decayed with the times. In that eclogue no contemporary poet is specifically named or blamed, and the ancients—Tityrus, Maecenas, and Augustus—are more symbolic than historical. For his contemporaries and himself Spenser has only generalizations, open questions, and indefinite pronouns:

The vaulting poets found nought worth a pease . . . (69)

O pierlesse Poesye, where is then thy place? . . . (79)

Whoever cast to compasse weightye prise . . . (103)

Furthermore, his security as an insider is such that he can include Elizabeth in the blame—"poesye is most fitt for 'Princes palace,'" but is not found there. Criticism in the service of committed love is appropriate to the ruler who Spenser knew loved him and her people.

In "Colin Clout," the lengthy passage on the state of poetry begins in the October mode—generalizations, open questions, indefinite pronouns:

Why? (said Alexis then) what needeth shee
That is so great a shepheardesse her selfe,
And hath so many shep*heards* in her fee,
To heare thee sing, a simple silly Elfe?
Or be the shep*heards* which do serve her laesie,
That *they* list not *their* mery pipes *applie*?
Or be *their pipes* untunable and craesie,
That *they* cannot her honour worthylie?
(368-75) (Emphasis added.)

Colin's answer, too, is evasive:

> Ah nay (said Colin) neither so, nor so:
> For better shepheards be not under skie . . .
> (377)

The shepherds are neither lazy nor incompetent. Colin explicitly rejects Alexis' reasons—"neither so, nor so"—but we note as well his reluctance to supply reasons of his own. Because Colin "cannot tell," Elizabeth must be the source of dissatisfaction. If she is the custodian of culture, why are able poets described with reference to her neglect? The passage reveals that Corydon is "meanly waged" (382), that Alabaster is not known to Cynthia as he ought to be, and that the Shepherd of the Ocean spends his wit in love's consuming smart, although his Muse could "empierce a Princes mighty heart." (Elizabeth is the prince, and the language is as excessive as that in Ralegh's lay.) Finally, Colin answers for a second time the question put to him earlier by Alexis. Why would Cynthia hear Colin sing? He is "a simple silly Elfe." His first answer is the correct pastoral answer. Colin says (ll. 358 ff.) that, though he was introduced to Cynthia by the Shepherd of the Ocean, the lady herself desired to hear him because she found his "simple song" "worth harkening to, emongst the learned throng." Country virtue humbles Eliza and shows her in her best light. Colin's second answer is contradictory and personal. He says:

> Yet found I lyking in her royall mynd,
> Nor for my skill, but for that shepheards sake.
> (454–55)

This verse seems closer to the truth. It frankly flatters Ralegh while raising the specter of a grudging Elizabeth who hears Spenser out to appease an angry suitor.

Following the catalogue of poets comes the first praise of Spenser's own beloved. Rosalind will now supplant Cynthia as object of private emotion; she, like Bregog and the sea journey earlier, has a discrete poetry. Colin addresses her directly in three sets of intricately related four-line verses; the key words "thought," "heart," "love," and "life" are repeated in the first line of the final quatrain:

> My thought, my heart, my love, my life is shee,
> And I hers ever onely, ever one:
> One ever I all vowed hers to bee,
> One ever I, and other never none.
> (475–78)

Although these lines are almost unreadable according to normal syntax, the effect is to force the reader to entwine Colin and his beloved forever. "Ever" (and "never") are used five times, "one" (and "onely") four times. This intricate, formal, yet personal poem embedded within the eclogue has little affinity with the praise of Eliza that follows; although a similar formality obtains in that piece, the protestations of interconnectedness between singer and ruler—Eliza bestowed "everie gift and everie goodly meed . . . everie day"—are little in evidence.

In the luxuriant first lines of Eliza's praise (l. 590) "words," "deeds," "looks," and "thoughts" are likened to "honny," "grapes," "sun beams," and "frankincense"; all is high pastoral, so high, in fact, that Eliza finds herself in heaven beholding "the cradle of her own creation."

> Emongst the seats of Angels heavenly wrought,
> Much like an Angell in all forme and fashion.
> (614–15)

Cuddy's response to this verse, actually a criticism of pastoral, simply confirms the reader's suspicions:

> Such loftie flight, base shepheard seemeth not,
> From flocks and fields, to Angels and to skie.
> (618–19)

Cuddy is correct; Colin makes no bridge from the usual pastoral ground —flocks and fields —to angels and sky. By using the plural, "Angels," Cuddy implies that angels do not belong in the poem, never mind Eliza's relation to them. Furthermore, poets should invoke one of two sets of conventions—flocks and fields or angels and sky—not both. The false note is, of course, Spenser's, but he cannot tell us its reason. He criticizes his own poetry rather than the queen, for whom he cannot find "true" pastoral words of praise.

While the first praise paragraph describes the unearthly beauty of Eliza, the second insists, in an English pastoral tone consistent with the opening lines of the poem, that trees, ground, stones, woods, waters, and even sheep will know her name, and shepherds' daughters dancing 'round will sing the poet's lays in praise of her. Monosyllables abound, and speaking woods and murmuring waters, easy pastoral phrases, appear. One phrase particularly stands out, though, not for its sentiment, which, like the passage, is standardized, but for its dissonance with the formal pastoral vocabulary. In the passage, Colin has already referred to his poetry living on after his own death:

> And when as Death these vital bandes shall breake,

Her name recorded I will have forever . . .
                    (630-31)

Some ten lines later the elegant locution personifying death is exchanged
for stark, English directness; the poet turns his *topos* of "brief life-eter-
nal art" into a simple encounter with his own mortality:

> And long while after I am dead and rotten:
> Amongst the shepheards daughters dancing round,
> My layes made of her shall not be forgotten . . .
>   (640-42)

Although one meaning is, as Thomas Edwards suggests, that Colin's
Platonic devotion to Elizabeth is confirmed by a "fully grasped image
of physical corruption"[30] —his poetry will survive him—as readers we are
less attentive to such ideal and conventional triumphs than we are to
Spenser's voice of human urgency. The words "dead and rotten" cause
us to mourn the coming of the poet's death. Singer and queen belong to
separate worlds, and Colin will not praise Eliza again. Rosalind takes
her place, but not until it becomes apparent in the final movement of
the poem that the pastoral frame is irreparably rent.

iv

One way to describe the narrative structure of "Colin Clout" and
its relation to city-country eclogue convention is to account for the es-
calation in tension that accompanies the periodic questions asked of
Colin. These questions function to move the poem along while simul-
taneously focusing the reader's attention on the pastoral construct itself
—that is, a history seen in retrospect where one is constantly reminded
by the presence of an audience within the poem (the attentive swains)
that the audience without (you, dear reader) should be jarred from its
habitual sophistication. Those naive questions should force the reader to
conclude that, for his own self-knowledge, "it is sometimes a good thing
to stand apart from your society so far as you can."[31]

> Corydon asks (200), "And is the sea so fearful? "
> Cuddy asks (290), "What land is that thou meanst . . ./And is there other, then
> where on we stand? "
> And Alexis (368) asks, ". . . What needeth shee . . . to heare/Thee sing, a simple
> silly Elfe? "

These questions (and there are others at regular intervals) reinforce the
goodness and simplicity of country singers. These singers behave as
though the clashing that we heard between the ideal realm and its

reality simply has not been heard by them; for them the poet's jour-
ney has conformed to convention.

Finally, Thestylis asks the pivotal question, a question of great mag-
nitude, one that is fundamental to the genre:

> . . . Why Colin, since thou foundst such grace
> With Cynthia and all her noble crew;
> *Why didst thou ever leave that happie place,*
> In which such *wealth* might unto thee accrew?
> (652–55) (Emphasis added.)

The paradox or logical puzzle of the poem, so long held at a distance,
can no longer be denied. Because Eliza is at the center, the poet has not
been able to diminish the golden world except indirectly. Because he
has not, those inside the poem—the naive questioners—finally contradict
the outsiders—the critical readers and the disappointed poet, who have
heard the intruding, unmasked voice. The constraints of genre have gone
awry. The swains now argue inappropriately against their guide Colin.
They still believe that court is the desirable place to be. Here is Thesty-
lis, naively and, perhaps, "truly," accusing Colin of spight and envy:

> Shepheard (said Thestylis) it seemes of spight
> Thou speakest thus gainst their felicitie,
> Which thou enviest, rather than of right
> That ought in them blameworthie thou doest spie . . .
> (676–79)

Colin argues back in a 50-line harangue that includes every conventional
abuse ever listed in court satire—deceit, slander, intellectual incompe-
tence, flattery, vanity. When Hobbinol argues back he mentions, surpris-
ingly, that he, too, has been at court, and thinks Colin's "blame . . . too
generall." One might, of course, propose that Spenser constructs the
poem this way to allow himself one final opportunity to diminish the
swains' naiveté, but I think not. Neither he nor the swains ever resolve
the court-country conflict. It is abandoned permanently, and Colin slips
obliquely into the long lecture on love that does not explain why he has
come home.

If the first 800 lines of the poem have been confusing by their incon-
sistency of tone and lack of firm control, the final 150 lines pose the
opposite problem; Colin is in complete control, but his birth as authori-
tative priest of love has no apparent link to what has come before. Cyn-
thia is never mentioned, and while the shepherds retain their role as
naive questioners, Colin appears to them as one inspired, a "vessel" for
"celestial rage," rather than as either swain or courtier. The city-county,

court-Ireland, high-low comparisons that bounded the world of the poem are abandoned for a world in which Colin makes absolute moral judgments.

At one point, for example, Colin says that Elizabeth's courtiers profane love's "mightie mysteries" by—and he lists sins against the sacred— "lewd speeches," "Licentious deeds," and using love's name idly and "in vaine." He addresses the god of love directly and asks, not forgiveness for them, but vengeance:

> Ah my dread Lord, that doest liege hearts possesse,
> Avenge they selfe on them for their abuses . . .
> (793-94)

Colin personally deplores this travesty of the most profound of private human emotions; although all love in the poem has been thwarted, none but court love has been insincere.

In his response Cuddy acknowledges Colin's heroic rage, and, importantly, does not question his authority about love, the private human emotion, although he had questioned Colin's authority about court. Cuddy says that Colin "shouldst bee Priest" of the god of love. In the lecture on love with which Colin answers him, he says he is priest. Like Milton's Raphael, Colin will interpret God's ways to man:

> Well may it seeme by this thy deep insight,
> That of that God the Priest thou shouldst bee
> So well thou wot'st the mysterie of his might,
> As if his godhead thou didst present see.
>   Of loves perfection perfectly to speake,
> Or of his nature rightly to define,
> Indeed (said Colin) passeth reasons reach,
> And needs his priest t' expresse his powre divine.
> For long before the world he was y'bore . . .
> (831-39)

And, finally, having dismissed the public court world, Colin establishes his own court, where he presides as love's chief justice. He concludes:

> Thus ought all lovers of their lord to deeme:
> And with chaste heart to honor him alway:
> But who so else doth otherwise esteeme,
> Are outlawes, and his lore do disobay.
> For their desire is base, and doth not merit,
> The name of love, but of disloyall lust:
> Ne mongst true lovers they shall place inherit,
> But as Exuls out of his court be thrust.
> (887-94)

With this passage the lecture on love closes. In the last 60 lines of the poem Ireland's pastoral landscape and conventional pastoral love find full expression, but we can, of course, no longer believe in it. The last passage quoted tells us why. If the intrusion of inappropriate phrases and unanswerable questions characterized the earlier movements of the poem, this final movement displays what we might explain today as an unconscious self-defense. In order to repair the injustices of Elizabeth's court and to build a defense against the disappointments he suffered personally in the public realm, Spenser creates and sets himself at the center of a private realm in his own mind. Those who do not honor and love "love" properly, he can there judge to be outlaws who should be exiled. He echoes in these lines a policy of exclusion he had earlier remarked at Elizabeth's court, but then he had been not judge but victim —the "gentle wit" "shouldered" "out of doore" (709). The irony of this position eludes recognition within the poem, but the reader without must notice that Spenser has seized, indirectly, the critical issue of his own life—his status as an exile from England. He is the literal "Exul," "thrust out" of court. He compensates for this status by exiling others from his private psychological world.

This reading of "Colin Clout" confirms exactly the meaning of the fleeting and mysterious vision of Colin piping on Mount Acidale in Book VI, Canto x of *The Faerie Queene*. In that vision Colin's piping controls, or is a condition for the reader being permitted to view, the hundred naked ladies, the graces, and Colin's "shepheardes lasse." But when Calidore does not enter the "pleasaunce" "For dread of them unwares to be descryde," we see that the two worlds are unaware of each other; the word "unaware" underscores their separation by modifying both Calidore and dancers. This is not the paradox it seems. When Calidore asks Colin why the graces fled from him, Colin answers by asserting his own special relation to the vision. He uses the familiar word "grace":

> For being gone, none can them bring in place,
> But whom they of themselves list so to grace.
> (VI, x, 20)

Spenser means that, although Colin owns the most "astonishing" poetic world of Book VI, this world of private grace has no enduring moral power in Calidore's social world. Calidore is unaware in that he is innocent. Colin's vision does not matter to his public world. Alpers rightly says of the vision that its meaning is not "determined by Calidore's dramatic relation to it. Although Calidore causes the Graces to disperse, the vision itself is in the world of Colin Clout."[32]

In the lecture on love Colin makes the law; in the story of Rosalind that ends the poem he shows that he can obey the law of his own making.

If he is not representative citizen, he can be representative lover, a true votary. A shepherd Lucid repeats a rumor he has heard of Rosalind's cruelty to Colin. Lucid has been a good student of Colin's theology of love, however; he asks the question and gives the answer:

> But who can tell what cause had that faire Mayd
> To use him so that used her so well:
> Or who with blame can justly her upbrayd,
> For loving not? For who can love compell?
> (911–14)

If Old Mole's daughter Mulla did love, and Rosalind does not, the correct aphorism is: "For who can love compell." The private world of love eschews failure. It is not analagous to court. Thwarted love is not like thwarted preferment.

And yet the retreat to private love is not a satisfactory poetic solution. If we ask again the relation between Colin's establishing his own court and what I have called "the pivotal question"—Why did Colin return home?—the failure of the poem can be teased out. Although the poem does make the requisite denial of Cynthia's ill disposition towards Colin, we do not believe it, and the world of the courtiers has been directly criticized. On the other hand, we have also been aware of the poem's contradictory attitudes towards Ireland. It is not just that Ireland represents "waste and hardness," a moral and geographical landscape where we find out what we are, but that it, too, is controlled by forces external to the poet—thieves, outlaws, starving, dispossessed marauders.

Although the poem ends back in the world of *The Shepheardes Calender* where pastoral landscape is again the whole landscape and anticipated death a convention for Colin's undying love, the metaphoric world is unconvincing. Given the puzzle and complexity of all that has come before, the human and contradictory "I" that guided us on our voyage cannot be suddenly reduced to Rosalind's "simple trophe." The cumulative experience of the poem denies our naive assent.

Notes

PREFACE

1. William Empson, *Some Versions of Pastoral* (New York: New Directions, 1950).
2. Albert Camus, *The Rebel.*
3. Leo Marx, "Susan Sontag's 'New Left' Pastoral: Notes on Revolutionary Pastoralism in America," *Literature in Revolution, TriQuarterly* (Illinois, 1972) 23/24, Winter/Spring, p. 555.
4. Empson, *Some Versions of Pastoral*, p. 11.
5. Ibid., p. 115.
6. Ibid., p. 6.

INTRODUCTION

1. All quotations from Spenser's works are from *Spenser's Faerie Queene*, ed. J. C. Smith (London: Oxford University Press, 1909) or *Spenser's Minor Poems*, ed. E. de Selincourt (London: Oxford University Press, 1910). The book, canto, verse, or line cited is indicated in the text.
2. Samuel Johnson, "The Life of Milton," *The Works of the Most Eminent English Poets* (London, 1779), vol. 2.
3. Empson, *Some Versions of Pastoral*, pp. 11, 12.
4. Ibid., p. 13.
5. Ibid., p. 72.
6. Frank Kermode, *English Pastoral Poetry* (New York: Barnes and Noble, 1952), p. 41.
7. Patrick Cullen, *Spenser, Marvell, and Renaissance Pastoral* (Cambridge, Mass.: Harvard University Press, 1970).
8. Paul McLane, *Spenser's Shepheardes Calender: A Study in Elizabethan Allegory* (Notre Dame, Ind.: Notre Dame University Press, 1961).
9. Isabel MacCaffrey, "Allegory and Pastoral in *The Shepheardes Calender*," *English Literary History* 36, no. 1 (1969): 88–109.
10. Kermode, *English Pastoral Poetry*, p. 37.
11. Cullen, *Renaissance Pastoral*, p. 26.
12. Ibid., p. 10.
13. T. E. Page, ed., *Bucolica et Georgica* (1898; London: Macmillan, 1963).
14. All translations from Peter Dale Scott, "Translation of Virgil" (Berkeley, Calif., 1969) (unpublished).
15. Paul Alpers, "The Eclogue Tradition and the Nature of Pastoral," *College English* 34 (1972): 353–71.
16. Ibid., p. 364.
17. Ibid., p. 364.
18. Ibid., p. 364.
19. MacCaffrey, "Allegory and Pastoral," p. 95.

143

20. Ibid., pp. 104, 105.
21. Empson, *Some Versions of Pastoral*, p. 19.

CHAPTER 1

1. "Epistle," *Spenser's Minor Poems,* ed. E. de Selincourt.
2. Kermode, *English Pastoral Poetry,* p. 41.
3. *The Works of Edmund Spenser: A Variorum Edition,* ed. Edwin Greenlaw et al. (Baltimore: The Johns Hopkins University Press, 1932-1957), vol. 1, pp. 332, 374.
4. In the first chapter ("The Pastoral Context") of *Spenser, Marvell, and Renaissance Pastoral,* Patrick Cullen establishes two pastoral strains: Arcadian and Mantuanesque. But because Cullen's interest is in a broad view of Renaissance pastoral, he separates his reading of *The Shepheardes Calender* from his reading of Mantuan, so that we remain without a careful analysis of Spenser's "borrowings" from Mantuan. Similarly, Cullen mentions Marot's pastoral only in a passing comment on the April eclogue; he does not explore Marot as a significant source for particular eclogues of *The Calender.*
5. Hallett Smith, *Elizabethan Poetry* (Cambridge, Mass.: Harvard University Press, 1952), p. 32. C. S. Lewis, in *English Literature in the Sixteenth Century* ([Oxford: Clarendon Press, 1954], p. 360), claims that Spenser had two groups of sources—both Renaissance—the "arcadian idealization . . . of Sannazaro and Guarini," and the "rough, superficially realistic" pastoral of Barclay and Mantuan.
6. This is the sentence with which American students of Latin begin their readings in ancient authors. Gaius Julius Ceasar, *Bellum Gallicum,* Book I.
7. Cited in Thomas Farnaby's edition of *Martial* (London, 1615); the reference appears in W. P. Mustard's "Introduction" to his edition of *The Eclogues of Baptista Mantuan* (Baltimore: The Johns Hopkins University Press, 1911), p. 39.
8. In *The Green Cabinet: Theocritus and the European Pastoral Lyric* (Berkeley: University of California Press, 1969), p. 21, Thomas Rosenmeyer defines the Hesiodic strain as: ". . . weighted down with the sweat and rewards of the peasant's life . . . the tradition is activist, critical, realistic." So too is the Georgic.
9. *The Eclogues of Alexander Barclay,* ed. Beatrice White (London: Early English Text Society, no. 175, 1928).
10. Alpers, "Eclogue Tradition," p. 355.
11. Virgil uses *doces* (you teach) in *Eclogue I.* The usage is strikingly similar to Spenser's, and indicates his careful reading of Virgil.
    nos patriam fugimus; tu, Tityre, lentus in umbra
    formosam resonare doces Amaryllida silvas.
    (4-5)
12. Horace, *Odes,* Book II, vii.
13. Renato Poggioli, "The Pastoral of the Self," *Deadalus* 88 (1959): 686-99.
14. Virgil, *Eclogue IV,* 11. 1-3:
    Sicelides Musae, paulo maiora canamus!
    non omnes arbusta iuvant humilesque myricae;
    si canimus silvas, silvae sint consule dignae.
15. Alpers, "Eclogue Tradition," p. 364.
16. By "medieval book," I mean the *topos* by which an idea is given authenticity by ascribing it to an authority—the Bible, an old book, an honored ancient.
17. Spenser would have known that the word *caelicolae* (VII, l. 59) means "gods" or "deities" in classical Latin. Thus his rejection of the hills themselves means that *despite* their godliness he prefers to see them as a touchstone to the saints rather than as holy heights—a notion that would give absolute value to highlands and highland dwellers.
18. The final pages of chapter 4 take up the theme of breaking human bonds in relationship to accumulating immoderate wealth.
19. Clement Marot, *Oeuvres Lyriques,* ed. C. Mayer (London: Athlone Press, 1964), pp. 343 ff.
20. When Virgil addresses a patron directly, as he does Varus in *VI* and Pollio in *VIII,* his deference exists only in asking the attention of his listener in the frame. The songs that follow

in each case are self-contained and the patrons do not appear in them in disguise as they do in Marot. Each person stands *in propria persona*. Virgil assumes, as Horace does, that his song is as valuable as and, obviously, more enduring than any human hero—that, in fact, song is the most important way of preserving the memory of heroism.

21. Marot, *Oeuvres Lyriques*, pp. 321 ff.
22. Empson, *Some Versions of Pastoral*, pp. 11, 12.
23. *The Prose Works of Sir Philip Sidney*, ed. A. Feuillerat (Cambridge: At the University Press, 1952), vol. 3, p. 17.
24. Ibid., p. 18.

CHAPTER 2

1. Both Northrop Frye, in "The Structure of Imagery in *The Faerie Queene*," *Fables of Identity* (New York: Harcourt Brace, 1963), and Paul Alpers, in "The Eclogue Tradition and the Nature of Pastoral," point to the self-description in this phrase. Alpers adds the wonderful note that stanza, of course, *means* "room" in Italian.
2. Smith, *Elizabethan Poetry*, p. 32.
3. Empson, *Some Versions of Pastoral*, p. 15.
4. Paul Alpers, *The Poetry of the Faerie Queene* (Princeton, N. J.: Princeton University Press, 1967), p. 13.
5. *Works of Edmund Spenser: A Variorum Edition*, vol. 1, p. 248.
6. A third meaning of waste, spelled "waist," is suggested by Gerald Willen and Victor B. Reed, editors of *A Casebook on Shakespeare's Sonnets* (New York: Thomas Y. Crowell, 1964), p. 131.
7. My language of the "resonating landscape" comes from "Imago Vocis in Vergilian Pastoral," a chapter of Phillip Damon's *Modes of Analogy in Ancient and Medieval Verse*, University of California Publications in Classical Philology (Berkeley, 1961), vol. 15, no. 6, pp. 281-98.
8. We should note, however, that Spenser decorously changes the sexes of the actors. He makes the rejecting beloved female and the castoff lover male.
9. *Prose Works of Sir Philip Sidney*, vol. 2, pp. 208-17.
10. Ibid., p. 212.
11. Smith, *Elizabethan Poetry*, p. 36.
12. Damon, *Modes of Analogy*, p. 289.
13. Ibid., p. 288.
14. Johnson denigrates *Lycidas* for its "trifling fictions" because the shepherds in question had no flocks to batten. (*The Works of the Most Eminent English Poets*, vol. 2.)
15. Smith, *Elizabethan Poetry*, p. 36.
16. Christopher Marlowe, "The Passionate Shepherd to his Love," *England's Helicon* (1614; London: Routledge and Kegan Paul, 1962), p. 192.
17. David Enelow, "The Wandering Mind and the Pastoral Imagination." Unpublished paper. (Berkeley, Calif., 1969.)
18. C. L. Barber, *Shakespeare's Festive Comedy* (Princeton, N. J.: Princeton University Press, 1959), p. 19.
19. These and the flower name etymologies that follow are taken from two sources: W. W. Skeat, *Etymological Dictionary of the English Language* (London: Oxford University Press, 1910) and Eric Partridge, *Origins: The Encyclopedy of Words* (New York: Macmillan, 1958).
20. Martha Craig, "The Secret Wit of Spenser's Language," in *Elizabethan Poetry*, ed. Paul Alpers (London: Oxford University Press, 1967), pp. 447-72.
21. Ibid. pp. 449, 451.
22. Ibid., p. 450.
23. Hugh Kenner, "Editor's Note," *Seventeenth Century Poetry* (New York: Holt, Rinehart and Winston, 1964), p. x.
24. "The Cuckoo Song" (c. 1230-40), ll. 9-10
25. The reader may be interested to note that the other flowers also fall into one of our two

categories: violet and pink are both rustic; Skeat tells us that for both "the name of the colour is due to that of the flower." Obviously, the dual associations they bring to the poem are flower image and color. Kingcups and coronations are rustic also; the first, of the genus *Ranunculus*, originates in the country fancy like the homely butter cup with which it is associated. The second is a corruption of a corruption—that is, "coronation" (meaning crowning) derives from "the flowers being 'dented or toothed like to a littal crownet' (Lyte)" so that its associations are in the rustic fancy, but it also seems to be connected with and a corruption of "carnation," a more learned name that Partridge (who disagrees with Skeat) thinks derived from "flesh tints." Chevisaunce, for which I do not find a listing, clearly has a French origin that must be connected to *cheval* and *chevalerie*. This flower name, then, must be a corruption of popular French. Cullambine and primrose, like daffodil, are corruptions of learned botanical names and, thus, belong to our second category, which makes a direct connection between flower and name. Cullambine or, more frequently, columbine, derives from LL *columbina*. There is a homely association, but it is Latin: "columbinus, of or like a *columba* or dove"—dove does not come to the surface in the English flower name. Primrose has a popular etymology in "prime" or "first" (early rose), but is, historically, a corruption of ME primerole and LL *primerula*. Finally, my botanical research tells me that carnations are double-petal pinks and belong to the class gillyflowers. Were we to assemble Spenser's bouquet, we should find its blossoms surprisingly repetitious; clearly, Spenser's interest is in association and variety in language.

26. Barber, *Shakespeare's Festive Comedy*, p. 32.
27. Empson, *Some Versions of Pastoral*, p. 69.
28. Ibid., p. 61.

CHAPTER 3

1. Illustrations of the June and August labors can be found in H. W. Janson, *The History of Art* (New York: Prentice-Hall, 1962), p. 253.
2. May is described and illustrated in Charles R. Morey, *Medieval Art* (New York: W. W. Norton Company, 1942), p. 285, fig. 114.
3. Janson, *History of Art*, p. 281.
4. Leo Spitzer, "Spenser, *Shepheardes Calendar, March*," Studies in Philology (Chapel Hill, N. C., 1950) vol. 47, pp. 494–505.
5. Ibid., pp. 494, 495.
6. Ibid., p. 496.
7. Ibid., p. 496.
8. Ibid., p. 499.
9. Smith, *Elizabethan Poetry*, p. 50.
10. Nowhere in Spenser does the end of childhood produce the radical cruelty that Marvell portrays as "little T. C.'s" future. The narrator of the poem will watch "from some shade" as the young woman whose eyes are "glancing wheels" drives "in Triumph over Hearts that strive."
11. Spitzer, "*Shepheardes Calendar, March*," p. 500.
12. David Kalstone, *Sidney's Poetry: Contexts and Interpretations* (Cambridge, Mass.: Harvard University Press, 1965), p. 77.
13. William Empson, *Seven Types of Ambiguity* (New York: New Directions, 1953), p. 43.
14. *Eclogue I*, ll. 24–25:
    verum haec tantum alias inter caput extulit urbes,
    quantum lenta solent inter viburna cupressi.
15. Smith, *Elizabethan Poetry*, p. 43.
16. Ibid., p. 43.
17. John Thompson, *The Founding of English Metre* (New York: Columbia University Press, 1961), p. 90.
18. Lewis, *English Literature in the Sixteenth Century*, pp. 360, 361.
19. Thompson, *The Founding of English Metre*, p. 108.
20. Ibid., p. 109.

21. Rosenmeyer, *The Green Cabinet*, p. 9.
22. (1614; London: Routledge and Kegan Paul, 1962), p. 11.
23. Stephen Orgel, *The Jonsonian Masque* (Cambridge, Mass.: Harvard University Press, 1965), pp. 6–7.

CHAPTER 4

1. Cited in A. G. Dickens, *The English Reformation* (New York: Schocken Books), p. 297.
2. Patrick Collinson's work *The Elizabethan Puritan Movement* (Berkeley: University of California Press, 1967) discusses these issues.
3. S. T. Bindoff, *Tudor England* (Baltimore: Penguin Books, 1950), p. 225.
4. Ibid., p. 241.
5. Ibid., p. 210.
6. Ibid., p. 224.
7. Dickens, *English Reformation*, p. 333.
8. William P. Haugaard, *Elizabeth and the English Reformation: The Struggle for a Stable Settlement of Religion* (London: Cambridge University Press, 1968), pp. 183 ff.
9. Ibid., p. 211.
10. Ibid., p. 209.
11. Ibid., p. 212. (Citing *Correspondence of Matthew Parker* [Cambridge, 1853].)
12. Bindoff (Citing Bishop Hutton, 1573), *Tudor England*, p. 227.
13. Ibid., p. 228.
14. Dickens, *English Reformation*, p. 313.
15. Collinson, *Elizabethan Puritan Movement*, p. 113.
16. *Op. cit.*
17. Collinson, *Elizabethan Puritan Movement*, p. 160. The clergyman was Thomas Sampson.
18. Ibid., p. 160.
19. Cited in McLane, *Spenser's Shepheardes Calender*, p. 143.
20. Ibid., p. 147.
21. Ibid., p. 148.
22. Barber, *Shakespeare's Festive Comedy*, p. 19.
23. Bindoff, *Tudor England*, p. 224.
24. Collinson, *Elizabethan Puritan Movement*, p. 201.
25. Haugaard, *Elizabeth and the English Reformation*, p. 205.
26. Spenser's images make men uncontrollably bestial. Even the anticlerical passage in Milton's "Lycidas" seems subdued by comparison because it does not turn men into animals, but, rather, indicts them as men who act "for their bellies' sake," who shove away "the worthy bidden guest," who make immoral human decisions.
27. T. E. Bottemore, ed., *Karl Marx: Early Writings* (New York: McGraw Hill, 1964), p. 192.
28. Ibid., p. 193.
29. Ibid., p. 193.

CHAPTER 5

1. Many critics have been puzzled by the fleeting vision of Colin in Book VI because the sensuous purity of the description of him seems dissonant within Calidore's narrative. Donald Cheney's is a typical view. He says that Calidore here encounters "the rejected pastoral mask of Spenser" (*Spenser's Image of Nature: Wild Man and Shepherd in "The Faerie Queene"* [New Haven, Conn.: Yale University Press, 1966], p. 2). He interprets the vision to represent the poet as "mediator between the two worlds of phenomenon and idea." It contrasts "the idealized world of impalpable images summoned by the music, and the humble grossly actual world into which they are summoned" (p. 230). Paul Alpers also suggests the vision's separation from Calidore's world by commenting that the "vision itself is in the world of Colin Clout" (*Poetry of The Faerie Queene*, p. 297). But, to my knowledge, no critics have linked the separateness of that vision with "Colin Clout's Come Home Againe." The vexed and contradictory Colin who appears in "Colin Clout" can go far toward explaining Spenser's

choice to present the Colin of Book VI in a self-contained, pure vision rather than as the failed dramatic actor he becomes in the real world of "Colin Clout."

2. Empson, *Some Versions of Pastoral*, p. 115.

3. April eclogue, *The Shepheardes Calender*, ll. 97–99.

4. I use "nonliterary" to distinguish between pastoral satire (or "hard" pastoral) and unmediated description of the social and material conditions of Spenser's life. Pastoral satire, or "hard" patoral, uses a landscape of winter and rough weather self-consciously to expose and criticize human nature; nonliterary description in "Colin Clout" rends the pastoral garment without intention, and is sensed by the reader as inappropriate, a violation of the poem's own aesthetic.

5. "Wretched" not only means "miserable," but derives from the misery of exile, an etymology Spenser would know. "Anglo Saxon *wrecca*, an exile, outcast, lit. 'one driven out'" (Skeat, *Etymological Dictionary*).

6. Stephen J. Greenblatt, *Sir Walter Ralegh: The Renaissance Man and his Roles* (New Haven, Conn.: Yale University Press, 1973), p. 55.

7. Ibid., p. 60.

8. Ibid., p. 51.

9. Thomas R. Edwards, "The Shepherd and the Commissar," *Imagination and Power: A Study of Poetry on Public Themes* (London: Oxford University Press, 1971).

10. C. S. Lewis, *English Literature in the Sixteenth Century*, p. 371.

11. The practice of "planting" colonies derives from the Romans, who early saw that stability in a conquered nation comes when the colonizers take up permanent residence and establish social and economic relations (marriages, particularly) with the indigenous population.

12. In the June eclogue of *The Shepheardes Calender*, Colin calls the pleasant *site* described by Hobbinol a blessed *state*. (See my introduction.)

13. A. L. Rowse, *The Expansion of Elizabethan England* (New York: Harper and Row, 1965), pp. 93, 94.

14. Cited in Rowse, *Expansion of Elizabethan England*, p. 93.

15. *Works of Edmund Spenser: A Variorum Edition*, p. 147. ("A View" was written in 1596, but remained unpublished until 1633, when its controversial analysis and recommendations were obsolete.)

16. Ibid., p. 54.

17. Isabel MacCaffrey, for one, calls the poem "a classic example of the pastoral paradigm" ("Allegory and Pastoral,", p. 137).

18. So, too, for the reality of *The Tempest*'s landscape or the Forest of Arden in *As You Like It*.

19. Here I follow Alpers' reading in *Poetry of the Faerie Queene*, p. 291–93.

20. William Empson says that "the feeling that life is essentially inadequate to the human spirit" is "naturally at home with most versions of pastoral" (*Some Version of Pastoral*, p. 114).

21. That Spenser intends his readers to make specific connections between the Colins of *The Shepheardes Calender*, "Colin Clout," and Book VI of *The Faerie Queene* is confirmed by the parenthetical question that introduces Colin in Book VI:

That jolly shepheard, which there piped, was
Poore Colin Clout (who knowes not Colin Clout?)
(x, 16)

22. Edwards, "Shepherd and the Commissar," p. 57.

23. Ibid., p. 51.

24. Ibid., p. 49.

25. Spenser repeats the aphorism later when, toward the end of the eclogue, Lucid defends Rosalind by saying, "Or who with blame can justly her upbrayd / For loving not? For who can love compell?" (914). The aphorism connects Mulla and Rosalind; both belong to the private world of love that is separate from the political world of court—a point discussed later in the chapter.

26. Critics note that the remaining fragments of "The Ocean to Cynthia" do not have the "undersong" that Colin describes but, still, it is an accurate rendering of Ralegh's style. There may be a lost version of the poem. Stephen Greenblatt makes this suggestion in *Sir Walter Ralegh*. pp. 60–61.

27. Greenblatt, *Sir Walter Ralegh*, p. 85.
28. *Works of Edmund Spenser: A Variorum Edition,* p. 158.
29. Ibid., p. 100.
30. Edwards, "Shepherd and the Commissar," p. 54.
31. Empson, *Some Versions of Pastoral*, p. 20.
32. Alpers, *Poetry of the Faerie Queene*, p. 297.

Index of Works and Passages

Page references for general discussions of works are cited first. References to lines in a specific work are in **boldface** type and are followed by references to pages containing a discussion of those lines.

Library of Congress Cataloging in Publication Data

Hoffman, Nancy Jo.
    Spenser's pastorals.

    1. Spenser, Edmund, 1552?–1599. The shepheardes
calender. 2. Spenser, Edmund, 1552?–1599. Colin Clout
3. Pastoral poetry, English—History and criticism.
I. Title.
PR2359.H6   821'.3   77–4540
ISBN 0–8018–1984–9